YOU DON'T WANT TO BE PUBLISHED

YOU DON'T WANT TO BE PUBLISHED

And Other Things Nobody Tells You When You First Start Writing

PETER M. BALL

Brain Jar Press
PO Box 6687
Upper Mt Gravatt, QLD, 4122
Australia
www.BrainJarPress.com

Copyright © 2018 Peter M. Ball

The moral right of Peter M. Ball to be identified as the author of this work has been asserted.

All rights reserved. No part of this book may be reproduced in any form or by any electronic or mechanical means, including information storage and retrieval systems, without written permission from the author, except for the use of brief quotations in a book review.

Cover design by Brain Jar Press
Cover Image: mika48/Shutterstock

ISBN: 978-0-6481761-4-5

Contents

An Introduction	vii
The Nine Business Mantras Of A Cranky Writer	1
You Don't Want To Be Published	14
Focus On the Mountain, Not the Map	27
Writing, Budgeting, and Shame	35
Lets Be Clear: I Know Fuck-All About Writing And Publishing (And That Means I Know A Lot)	41
How To Process Publishing Advice, Part One: Use What Works	47
How To Process Writing Advice, Part Two: Diversity Your Sources	54
There Is Nothing Surprising About A Writer Getting Rejected (Even J.K. Rowling)	58
5 Reasons Rejection Letters Are Actually Awesome	64
Yes, You Are Wasting Your Time As A Writer	70
The First Rule of Write Club	77
The Incredible Sucker-Punch of Success	86
Networking Tips for Reclusive, Introverted Writer-Types	95
How To Get the Most Out Of An SF Con As An (Introverted) Emerging Writer	104
Al Snow's Advice For SF Writers	113
Patreon, Tools, Tactics, and Strategy	123
Links	133
About the Author	139

An Introduction

OR "WHY I HELL AM I LISTENING TO THIS GUY?"

Three things you'll want to know before we go on.

First, there's a bunch of essays about *being* a writer in these pages, but very little specifically about the *craft* of writing. Folks who are looking to learn the techniques for writing a short story or novel are well-served by a plethora of existing books, blogs, and workshops, in addition to author talks and conferences. Writers talk craft the way most people breathe, because it's easier and considerably more fun than discussing the minutia and mundane realities of running the small business every writer becomes as their career develops.

Given my background, I tend to spend more time on the other half of being a writer: building a career; figuring out the next step once the story or book is done. All the shit that's a lot more complicated than actually putting words on paper, because there's all this mythology and muddled-headed thinking about "being creative" and "being a successful writer" that gets in the way of doing a good job.

Second: I swear a lot in these essays, and I mean a whole fucking lot. For some people that's a dealbreaker, so

I give you fair warning up front. If you're upset by cursing that's occurred thus far, things will only get worse. This book is probably not for you.

Finally, a short introduction for those who are unfamiliar with my work.

My name is Peter M. Ball, and I've spent the bulk of my adult life either writing for a living or working jobs where I taught people how to write or navigate the field of publishing and get their work out there.

Over the years I've taught writing courses for universities and writers centres, convened four instalments of the GenreCon writers conference here in Australia, spent five years managing the *Australian Writers Marketplace* for the Queensland Writers Centre, and published a whole lot of short stories, poems, articles, gaming books, and novellas. I've been a paid blogger, a copy writer, and a very grouchy mentor. Now, I'm a small press publisher, putting out books with the goal of changing the way we tap about creativity.

In recent years, I've started taking the things I talked about at work and transforming them into essays, blog posts, and articles. Some of these were routinely shared by writers, agents, or editors who are a considerably bigger deal than I am, which often convinces people I know a few things about this gig.

Despite all of this, you probably haven't heard of me. That's how writing careers go for most people. Not every writer becomes a household name, even if they've been making their career out of words for nearly twenty years.[1]

While I know a few things and share my thoughts and experiences pretty freely, I'm not a guru by any stretch. What I offer here is the best advice I have on some very complicated subjects, but they're often things to think about carefully rather than step-by-step guides telling you everything you need to know.

Treat me as the one-true-expert at your goddamned peril, is what I'm saying, but this is true of every damn writer who offers you advice. There are lots of ways to write, and there are lots of ways to have a writing career. No advice is one-size-fits-all, especially these days.

Writing and publishing are now very different businesses than they were when I started writing in the nineties. I expect they'll have changed even more by the time I stop banging out words and start pushing up daisies. This means it's a very strange time for folks who *talk* about writing and publishing, because there's multiple viable paths for people looking to achieve their goals and all of the can be right — or wrong — depending on individual circumstances.

In this environment, good advice gets you working in the industry as it is, but great advice builds your capacity to understand why it works *even after the industry has changed*.

If I'm honest, this book is one of those changes in action: the sixteen essays included here got their start on my blog, *Man Vs. Bear*, although some of them were reprinted or adapted into magazine articles after they were posted. I've collected them together because some regular readers requested an easy reference for some of the frequently visited posts, and modern technology makes it easy to provide that.

The entries have been copy-edited to correct mistakes and rewritten to account for the fact that this is book, rather than a blog, but links to the originals are included in the back of the book. Please drop by if you'd like to see the originals, or drop a question into the comment threads. In addition, I've added a post-script to every entry, a little

2018 Commentary that provides additional context or extra thoughts to the topic du jour.

With that, let's get on with things. The good stuff awaits, and there's writing to be done.

Peter M. Ball
January 9, 2018

---

1. I'll admit, some of those years were *hard* years, and it would have been smarter to find another way to make a living, but I'm stubborn as hell.

The Nine Business Mantras Of A Cranky Writer

ORIGINALLY POSTED JULY 27, 2014

So here's the thing: I spend the vast majority of my daylight hours talking to aspiring writers about what they'd like to achieve and how they can get there. This is one of the things that comes with the territory when you work at a place like Queensland Writers Centre, and it's pretty sweet gig. You get to meet up-and-coming writers as they're getting their shit together and help them along the way; you get to meet older, established writers and glean what you can from their experience. You get to talk to the absolutely raw rookies, the people who have just decided *I want to be a writer* and want to know what they should do next.

When I answer questions at work, I'm polite and enthusiastic and eager to give you the best answer I can. I do so because that's what "work Peter" does.

This essay isn't written by the guy that's politely answers your queries if you call us at the centre. No, this is written by the guy who actually does the hard yards of sitting down and writing stuff; the grumpy-as-shit professional who spends the *other* half of the day trying to earn some extra cash out of his writing.

'Look,' that cranky writer snarls, 'this writing shit isn't that difficult. I can tell you everything you need to know with nine fucking rules. Just read those and go away; I've got a deadline looming.'

If you ask me about writing outside of work, and I'm inclined to help you, odds are the cranky writer is whose advice you're going to get. A list of mantras I find myself muttering during the particularly bad days at the keyboard, or when people who are close friends ask about writing and I don't feel the need to treat them with kid gloves.

Consider them rules to live by, if you're planning on being writer who wants to earn money from their work.

MANTRA ONE: I WILL TREAT MY FUCKING BUSINESS LIKE A BUSINESS

Somewhere along the line we convinced ourselves that publishing was a business and writing was a calling, which excused aspiring writers from ever having to put a moment's thought into how they should handle their careers. It's like we bought into the idea that publishers and agents handled all the business shit, while writers traipsed along sunlit meadows waiting for the muse to bequeath genius upon them.

Fuck that shit.

Writing is a business. The number of people I've seen make expensive fucking mistakes because they don't realise that is staggering. It never occurs to them that they should read their contracts, let alone negotiate the terms on a short story or article; or they mistake getting published for the end goal, instead of setting a goal like *build a sustainable career* and acknowledging that getting published is a single step towards it.

The truth is this: if you're trying to be a writer and you're trying to get paid for your work, you are running a fucking business. Treat that with the respect it deserves, and focus on developing your business sense alongside you writing craft.

MANTRA TWO: I WILL HAVE A FUCKING PLAN

Most people, when they start a small business, put together a business plan that outlines useful stuff like *why they're starting this business,* and *how they're going to make money with the business,* and *what they expect to happen in the future.* Often it includes helpful marketing details like *why are we different to everyone else doing this kind of thing?*

The business plan helps them make decisions and allocated limited resources, provides day-to-day guidance about what's important, and generally helps keep things focused.

I can't blame people for shying away from planning. I mean, how many of us have heard the following when we say 'I'm a writer'?

- 'There's no money in writing.'
- 'But what's your real job?'
- 'Have you published anything I might have heard of?'
- 'You should go write something like Harry Potter and make millions!'
- 'There are only three people making their living from writing in Australia.'

The rhetoric around writing seems to suggest that your

business plan for becoming a full-time writer is rather like winning the lottery — it's so rare that it just doesn't happen, and it moves success well outside of the things you can control.

This mindset doesn't go away when you become a working writer, either. Very few authors ever examine the trajectory of their own careers, let alone ask themselves how their choices affected where they ended up. And so they offer the advice based on their own experience, and that advice can be a poor fit for someone else.

Consider this: when I was doing a creative writing degree at university, the assumed "business plan" I inherited from the other professionals in my faculty was *write a novel, win the Vogel prize, get a teaching gig once your PhD is finished*. This is how most of my lecturers had built their career, and they couldn't point at many full-time writers as a counter-example. One of my tutors rolled out the canard that there are only three full-time writers in Australia, and we shouldn't assume we'd be one of them.

Now this makes perfect sense in a university environment, where the people who teach the courses are usually academics first and writers second. There are exceptions — rare exceptions — but the vast majority of academics in writing courses *aren't* making their career out of fiction. Their business model is being an academic first, and using that to support their writing.

And there is absolutely nothing wrong with that.

But here's the thing: if there are only three people making a full-time living out of their writing in Australia, I know them all. Plus some extras. And that's just among the writers who write science fiction and fantasy.

People do make a living out of this writing thing, which means you can go out and figure out *HOW* they're making a living. In reality, we're dealing with lots of different ways, since very few of them hit full-time-writing in exactly the same way. There might not be one sure path to a full-time writing career, but there are a wealth of options and approaches you might want to try.

So look to the writers whose careers you admire, and in particular the careers you'd like to emulate. Pay attention to the things they say about building their career, but also *what they did*, because the advice writers give isn't always an exact match for their lived experience or the current shape of their career.[1]

Because here's the thing: if you can figure out how they did it, rather than focusing on what they *say* they did, you can put together a plan that suits your goals and temperament. It may be more work than you want. It may still need a little luck to put you in the right place at the right time. It may even involve taking a close look at your dream and figuring out how realistic it is.

It may even teach you that you don't fucking want to write full-time, because it's a hard life and nowhere near as "creative" as folks assume.[2]

Writers tend to dream big and think small. We plan through to the end of our current project, figure we'll work out everything after that. Very rarely do I talk to people who are thinking five, ten years ahead. Fewer still have long-term dreams like *I'd like to quit my job and write* with a feasible plan behind them.

Don't be that writer. Have a fucking plan. If you're among the handful of writers who have never read Jeff VanderMeer's *Booklife*, go track down a copy. It will lead you through the planning side of things far better than I can, and give your writing career energy you never knew you had.

MANTRA THREE: I WILL KNOW WHAT I AM FUCKING SELLING

If you go into writing novels and short-stories without a basic understanding of copyright, how it works, and how writers make their income from carving up the permissions associated with their works, then you're in trouble.

If you're looking at the rise of ebooks and thinking, 'yeah, I'd like to experiment with that,' rather than looking at the *freely available data* about how people are making substantial incomes with ebooks, then you're in trouble.

If you're a writer of any type, and you've never looked into some of the ways of making money out of *being a writer* rather than your work itself, then you're missing out on a slice of income.

Once you start treating your business like a fucking business and focus on the plan, then next thing to look at is how you make money. The traditional ways, the new ways, and the ways you've never even thought about 'cause the opportunities weren't there.

I've worked for small businesses that didn't know what they were selling before. They could tell you what they did, and maybe even how, but rarely why we did it or how it added up to long-term growth and income. And they muddled along for a while, then … well, they died. Or they kept muddling along, sustained by the passion of the people running them, but the lack of focus meant their income sources never remained steady. Often, they were nightmare employers and frequently steered toward toxic work environment because of the ambient stress in the air.

Focus matters. You need to know what you're selling because sooner or later you're going to need to make hard decisions about how you use your time. Do I write a short story or work on a novel? Do I work on my novel, or prepare this course that will earn me a couple of hundred bucks? Do I keep writing fiction, or take the gig writing corporate copy for six times the money?

The answers to these can be deceptive. A corporate writing gig may give you a huge chunk of money now, but it only pays once. Stories and books earn less money upfront, but they're assets you own and they have the potential to keep earning for years to come. Neither is inherently the *wrong* choice, but the right choice will depend on your goals, circumstances, and business plan.

Having a real sense of where your money is coming from helps you decide how to allocate your time, how to evaluate the risks of each decision, and which opportunities will move you forward in the long run.

MANTRA FOUR: I WILL TRACK MY FUCKING RIGHTS

This is related to point three, but deserves its own datapoint simply because of how ridiculously fucking useful it is, yet no-one really does it. Track your damn rights.

Writers talk a lot about tracking submissions, knowing where you've submitted something and what the response was, but our attention tends to die off once the acceptance has come. The story or novel has done its job by then; we've been published, we've been paid.

Don't be that kind of writer. Fire up Excel and start a document where you track the rights of every story or novel or article you've sold. Have you sold first world English language rights? Write it down, along with the date when things revert. Did they take the audio rights? The ebook rights? Make a note of those too.

If you can't figure out what rights a being granted in

the contract, don't sign the contract. Go back. Negotiate. Be clear. It's a business transaction, after all, and this is worth getting right.

Filling all these details in may feel stupid when you've only got one short story published. It gets a lot less stupid when you're thirty stories in, with a handful of novellas, and you've got emails asking if you'd be willing to sell the translation rights to one story to a small press in Serbia right as an anthology editor is looking to reprint that story you wrote four years ago.

Sure, you could dig out your contracts to check, but having the one document makes life easier. If you're smart and proactive, it's also a tool that informs you it's time to reactivate a story and start searching for reprint markets, audio markets, and more.

MANTRA FIVE: I WILL RESPECT MY FUCKING AUDIENCE

You are not smarter than your audience. Your time is no more valuable. Your readers owe you nothing. If you don't deliver, they are well within their rights to fuck off and let you bleat about your work into the darkness.

When you write something, give it the attention and seriousness it deserves. When you are asked to write something, even if you find the topic faintly absurd, give it your best attention. If there are constraints based on time or topic or word-length, over-deliver as best you can within those limitations.

The moment you take your audience for granted, you've lost them. At best, they'll disappear. At worst, they'll sit in the audience of your reading and daydream about carving up your face with the sharp end of a beer bottle.[3]

MANTRA SIX: I WILL BACK UP MY FUCKING WORK

You do not back up your work enough. I don't care who you are, it's the truth. Every time you think your back-up system is impregnable, something will happen to remind you that there is still a hole there, somewhere, and you'll find yourself losing data.

You don't want to lose data. That data is stories and novels and articles. That data is the stuff you make your income from.

I've got a pretty good back-up system. It's not perfect, 'cause no system is ever perfect; there are always holes, no matter how automated the process. I've learned that twice this year. First, back in March, when the combination of being on holidays one week and being on deadline the next let to my computer being disconnected from its usual back-up systems.

I plugged that hole. Made sure it'd never happen again.

Then I lost my USB on the way home from Write Club one week. Four hours of work gone, but they were four really productive hours. Several thousand words down the drain.

You do not back up your work enough. No-one ever does. But you want to minimise the losses when things do go wrong, so institute the most stringent back-ups you can and then do a little more.

MANTRA SEVEN: I WILL HONE MY FUCKING CRAFT AND BUSINESS SKILLS

I know fuck-all about writing, really. I've done okay with what little I know – a couple of novellas, a shit-load of stories and poems, the bulk of my life spent working as a freelancer and contractor instead of going to an office (and when I broke that streak, it was to work on a games convention with a writer-focused panel stream, and then a writer's centre where I get to talk to writers constantly).

But I still maintain that I know fuck-all about writing, 'cause I'm realistic enough to know that there's always something new to learn and I want to stay hungry.

I am always looking to improve my craft. I owe it to my readers to be a better writer than I was on my last project; I owe it to myself to run my business better than I did last year. My guiding principle is always *I want to be better.*

Always be learning, whether it's through courses or books or just putting together a plan for figuring shit out. Get better at what you do. Admit that the skills that got you to this point aren't always the same skills that will get you to the next level, and prepare accordingly.

MANTRA EIGHT: I WILL GET MY SHIT DONE

I write my blog posts on the weekend. This seems ideal, but some weekends I'm sick and burnt out, which makes writing a week's worth of blog posts much less fun than you'd think. It doesn't matter. I'm the cranky writer. I will get my shit done.

Getting shit done is the basis of being a writer. I can't post blog entries that aren't written. I can't sell stories that aren't finished. I can't make money on a book that isn't finished and out there in the world.

It's easy to get distracted from this. The business of writing will distract you with emails and opportunities and planning, all of which feels like work. The internet will be there, asking you to waste time on Facebook. You will have a bad day. Your day job will eat time like no-ones business.

Your loved ones have perfectly reasonable expectations that you'll spend time with them, every now and then.

It doesn't matter. Get your shit done. If you're planning on writing for a living, writing is something that needs to get done.

MANTRA NINE: I WILL GET MY FUCKING HUSTLE ON

When I'm in Cranky Writer mode, there is a line between "a writer" and "someone who writes".

The writer hustles. They keep moving forward, like a shark. They line up projects. They think ahead. They're in it for the long haul, aware that writing is a long game. They know how the things they're doing now will connect to the things they want to do in five or ten years time.

They focus on the hustle, 'cause that's what being a writer is all about. They may not be making a living from their writing, but they have a strategy that's informed and workable. They look for ways to do new things with the work they've already done. They look for opportunities in things that have nothing to do with writing. They have a faintly manic gleam in their eye.

There are some damned fine writers who don't hustle. It's not a mandatory skill for writing well, but you learn to recognise it in the way a lot of full-time writers talk about building their careers.

If you want to be a Writer – a capital-W writer who actually makes income from their work — get your fucking hustle on. Give a damn about what you're doing. Pay attention to your business and hustle to make it work.

2018 COMMENTARY

I wrote this a few years into my writers centre gig, right about the point that I realised something very important: my default assumption, in every conversation about writing, is that people are trying to make a living at it.

Turns out, not everyone wants that. There are plenty of people who just want to write a memoir, or a single novel, and get back to the rest of their life. They need a different set of advice to everyone else, because it will never be their business.

I struggled to help those people, at first, because the mindset was so foreign to the way I'd learned to write.

On the other hand, there's also a large number of people who *say* they'd like to be a writer, then balk at the work required to do it. They're focused on the joy of creating, and overlook the fact that writers are effectively small businesses once they start earning money from their work.

Often this means they become poorly run small businesses, where all the focus is on the creative work instead of the planning and administration that goes with it.

That shit can kill your career momentum in all sorts of ways. I speak from experience here: there are writers who keep getting gigs with the centre because they answered their email in a timely manner, instead of treating it like an afterthought.

And while I wrote this before online services like Dropbox and Google made it easy to synchronise your work across multiple hard drives, you still aren't backing up your work enough.

Yes, even if you're using one of those systems.

---

1. Consider, for example, a writer like fantasy author Neil Gaiman, whose brand is a mix of writing-celebrity and celebrating the wonder and magic of stories. It's easy to look at the state of his career *now* — releasing books every few years to critical acclaim — and overlook the years spent working in journalism, writing monthly comics, and building a diverse network of contacts in the comics and publishing industry.
2. I've done it before, and I much prefer the part-time writer life, where every choice about what I'm writing isn't guided by whether or not it will pay my mortgage.
3. Yes, that example is enormously specific. It comes from attending a reading where four-fifths of the writers scheduled to perform had neglected to rehearse. One was so drunk they basically rambled in-jokes at their friends for twenty minutes, not bothering to present something the rest of the audience could understand.

   We'd given up time and money to see those fuckers, and I still hold a grudge against them because they'd failed to respect that.

You Don't Want To Be Published

ORIGINALLY POSTED JUNE 14, 2014

No-one tells you this when you're starting out, but here's a hard truth every aspiring writer should acknowledge: *you don't want to be published*.

Of course, you think I'm wrong. Most writers do. They put work into getting their manuscripts together *because* they want to be published. They develop their craft, and learn to redraft, *because* they want to be published. They submit, and keep submitting, *because* they want a publisher to say yes and publish their work. If they've been at it for a while, clocking up the rejections, getting published can feel like the most important goddamn thing in the world.

And still, I'm going to sit here and tell you that you're wrong. You don't want to be *published*, not really. Those words are just a shorthand, a way of deflecting attention from what you really want.

If you're trying to get your work published, what you really want is actually far more complex and harder to articulate than you know right now.

THE FOOLPROOF PLAN FOR GETTING PUBLISHED

I spent six years working at Queensland Writers Centre, a non-profit organisation here in Australia that helps new and emerging writers build their career. My job revolved around talking to new writers about the publishing process, telling them how to get their work out there. Nine times out of ten, when someone asked a question, it was *how do I get published?*

The job was complicated by the fact that the industry changed around me. Once upon a time the advice for getting published was easy to deliver, because traditional publishing dominated and we lacked viable alternatives. Then the internet came along, and ebooks, and the proliferation of phones and tablets. Indie publishing was a viable choice for certain types of writers, but people tended to treat it as thought going indie or through a traditional publisher were exactly the same.

In truth, they're very different business models with very different routes to success.

Over the space of six years I tried to talk people through the decisions about indie or traditional paths. I answered their question over the phone, in seminars, in person, and in magazine articles. Now I'm doing it here, and I'm sharing the one truth I've learned during those six years and nearly a decade of teaching creative writing classes before that. The secret that all writers know, but never truly say out loud.

You don't want to be published. No-one does. And here's how I know: getting published is easy. So easy, in fact, that I can offer you an absolutely foolproof plan that will get you published before the day is out.

Just follow these three easy steps:

1. Go to wordpress.com.
2. Fire up a new, free blog.
3. Post your work to the blog and hit publish.

Do those three things and boom, you're published. If that's truly all you wanted, you can now fuck off to the pub for a celebratory beer.

Odds are, your first response to the plan isn't joy and wonder. Most writers object when I lay it out. They start arguing and adding caveats, including my favourite: 'Yeah, but being published on a blog isn't really published, is it?'

I might not feel like it to you, but in the realities of the publishing industry, it definitely is. Many short story magazines and publishes won't look at work that's been published on a blog as an original submission, arguing that it's already seen publication and can only be treated as a reprint. In their mind, published on a blog is *published*, and there's no way to argue them around.[1]

People are loathe to accept the idea because blog publication doesn't really fit their idea of what being published *means*. If you listen to their arguments about *why* it shouldn't count, you start getting some insight into the thing they're really after when they're asking for advice. Consider the hidden intent lurking in the shadows of these objections:

- Yeah, but how do I make money from a blog?
- Yeah, but how do I find readers?
- Yeah, but how much effort will it take to make a blog work compared to other forms of publishing?

All those *Yeah, buts* are where the real desires start leaking out.

THE JOURNEY AND THE GOAL

So here's the thing: people mistake getting published for their goal, when really it's just one step towards the thing they really want. We use *getting published* as shorthand because it sounds so much cleaner, and it seems more achievable (and less egotistical) than articulating the things we're actually chasing with our writing.

That's fine if you're aware that it's short-hand, but mistaking a step on the journey for the goal frequently opens people up to all sorts of mistakes. It leads people towards the assumption that all publications are equal, which is when they start building a career in ways that don't match their true ambitions.

For some writers, this can result in costly mistakes, like working with a vanity publisher who will happily take their money to produce a book then do fuck-all to help them find an audience.

For others, it's a tendency to waste time chasing their career down blind alleys as they make decisions based on flawed assumptions (like giving work away "for exposure," or submitting to low-paying fiction markets first under the assumption they need to build their way up to the well-paying gigs).

For others, its self-publishing their book and assuming it will do as well as a traditionally published book, failing to take into account that publishers do more than produce the physical book and get it into bookshops. Self-publishers and traditional publishers leverage very different tools, and earn money on fundamentally different assumptions.

The other problem — and this is somewhat more drastic — is that lying to yourself about what you really want from writing can actually take the fun out of being published. You invest so much hope and desire in the first thing you have out, and it ends up feeling a little ... well, empty. The vast majority of books don't make their author famous, nor do they attract thousands of dollars or legions of adoring readers.

Some books do, sure, but they're outliers. Like hitting the jackpot in the lottery. Truth is, most books do okay numbers. Some books don't even do that.

It's never a happy day when your book or story doesn't do as well as you'd hoped, but it's a lot less demoralising when you recognise that book or story is just one step on a very long path. Most writing goals take years of cumulative effort and multiple publications to achieve, and a failed book is only the end if you truly believed that getting published was all it took.

Please, don't be that writer.

Few people put much thought into what they want from writing – generally, writers are pretty reactive bunch, simply doing whatever comes next – so figuring out what you really want from this gig can go a long way towards keeping yourself motivated on the weeks when writing is kicking your ass.

SO, WHAT DO YOU REALLY WANT WHEN YOU SAY "TO GET PUBLISHED"?

Man, figuring that out is the trick. In George Orwell's *Why I Write*, he put forth the argument that there are four impulses behind the desire to write and be read: sheer egotism; aesthetic enthusiasm; historical impulse; and political purpose. The proportions may be different in each of us, but some combination of those impulses guide nearly everything a writer chooses to do.

Personally, I'm not quite sold on Orwell's breakdown, although I'll admit to a sizeable degree of egotism behind my desire to get work out there. What I have noticed is a tendency towards certain themes after six years talking to aspiring writers, so I'll talk through them in more detail.

'I WANT A CAREER.'

The most common reason people want to get published is the desire to have a writing career or walk away from a day job (note: these are two different things). The *how* of this is rarely thought about: some people are so ill-informed about the realities of writing and publishing that they assume all writers are making *Harry Potter* money or that having a writing career is impossible 'cause no-one pays for writing. Sometimes, they believe both simultaneously, failing to recognise the irony.

In either case, the theory seems to be: *publish one book and quit my job.* When that doesn't work, it's assumed that publishing has crashed so badly it no longer supports writers rather than a fundamental problem with their approach.

Truthfully, these folks are usually the easiest to give advice too. You can educate them about the realities of the publishing business. You can point them towards all sorts of writers who make their career as a living and resources for improving their craft. And when it comes to the *I want to get published* statement, you can give them a goal to work towards: Five books.

This number was offered by agent Donald Maas in his book, *Writing the Breakout Novel.* He suggests that getting five novels published roughly coincides with the point where you can see how many readers will follow an author from book to book. I've heard some older writers suggest the number is closer to ten, and indie publishers throw around numbers like twenty or thirty,[2] but the point is largely the same.

Few writing careers are built on one or two books, but this doesn't stop frustrated writers disappointed by the low advance on their second or third novel from writing angry essays or think-pieces about the death of publishing or the difficulties of making a living as a full-time author.

In truth, your second book just means you're getting started. Start thinking about five books as the minimum you need to quit your job. Or ten books. Or thirty. Recognise that swapping genres will mean you need more books, as will long delays between releases. And recognise that going indie means it takes longer to find an audience, which is why so many of the indie strategies focus on writing fast, releasing often, and building up a backlist.

This isn't always a comfortable thing to hear, if you're pinning your hopes on writing a single book and achieving Harry Potter levels of success. Such things still happen in publishing, but it's not something to bank on.

If you're serious about wanting a career based on the written word, it's time to recognise that long-term careers and large bodies of work are often connected for a reason.

'I WANT AN AUDIENCE.'

The second-most common goal hiding behind *I want to be published* tends to be the desire for an audience. Particularly in the non-fiction and memoir crowds, and the *my fiction will change the world* types, there is an enormous hunger to tell stories and have them heard by a lot of people.

Some want it 'cause they believe they've written something that will legitimately help the world; some just want to be the literary equivalent of a rock star. There's a reason Orwell put *Sheer Egoism* at the beginning of his list of writer's motivations, and decades of working with aspiring writers has done nothing to convince me he's placed it in the wrong spot.

These people also get the five books advice mentioned above, plus all sorts of advice about author platform and engaging with an audience. Ironically, many of them probably should fire up a blog[3] and start posting regularly, since connecting with readers is easier than it's ever been. It takes time and a commitment to learning a new set of skills, but there are plenty of writers who have earned their audience online and used it to find a publishing deal.

Some have even found their book audience far less satisfying than their online audience.

'I WANT FAST MONEY.'

There are people who legitimately believe that getting published is the path to getting rich quick. People who work in publishing tend to laugh at the suggestion, since we know how well these gigs actually pay, but the misconception persists for a reason.

Take a moment to consider where the average person learns about the writing industry.

When writers pop up in the media it's because they've either achieved something out-of-the-ordinary, or because they're writers who are so famous that everything they do is news. This means we hear about things like John Scalzi signing a 3.4 million dollar deal for 13 books with Tor, or they're interviews with highly successful best-sellers like Stephen King, Stephanie Meyer, Robert Paterson, or JK Rowling. We never hear about the advances of the vast majority of writers, which are typically a few thousand dollars, unless it's being presented as a 'look at how little writers actually earn' tragedy.

The presentation of fictional writers are no better. When a writer appears in a film or movie, they're either an aspiring writer whose achieved nothing, or they are characters like Rick Castle from *Castle* or Carrie Bradshaw from *Sex in the City*. In short, writers who have done nothing and yet hope to make it big, or writers who are already big and successful in ways that can rarely be replicated in most writing careers. I'm still trying to figure out how Bradshaw afforded New York Rent on a columnists salary.

Basically, most new writers do not have access realistic examples of how writers make money. In fact, the entire process seems shrouded in mystery until you really start looking at the ways full-time writers keep their head above water.

Most people who seem to be asking this question get advised to look at alternatives. You *can* make fast money with writing if you're willing to hit up content mills, freelancing sites, and business writing, but it's rarely *good* money when you're starting out and building a portfolio, and it's not what most aspiring writers consider to be the fun stuff.

The money for fiction is much slower to come, and usually less than you're thinking up front, which brings us back to the importance of writing more and building up your audience.

'I WANT THE LIFESTYLE.'

What lifestyle? It changes from person to person, but there's definitely a streak of people who see aspects of the writer's job that they think they'd enjoy.

I've talked to people who wanted to earn writing income because it meant they weren't location dependent, while others enjoyed the idea of working for themselves and figured this was something they'd be good at. Some turned to the arts because they were looking to connect with a certain kind of person, and the arts were usually a signifier that they were among their tribe.

Others rhapsodise about the freedom to "be creative," which is the kind of thing that makes me clench my teeth so I don't say anything impolite. People entertain strange ideas about the realities of the freelance writing life, and the reality of being a small business focused on selling the written word is often more stressful than creative.

The trick with this one is to start getting specific about what aspects of the lifestyle you're really looking for. Even more important is figuring out whether writing is the best way to get it, which often means research and evaluating other writers processes and income streams so you can figure out what to replicate.

'I REALLY DO JUST WANT TO PUBLISH THIS ONE THING, THEN GO AWAY.'

A relative minority of people really do just want to publish the one thing they've written, then go back to their ordinary lives. Often, they're writing for small or discrete communities and have very specific goals, but they phrase their queries in the same way as everyone else because they don't realise that they're different.

These folks may still have concerns about the size of their audience or the money they earn, but ultimately they're just looking for the best deal they can get for their one thing, rather than talking through the various options available.

Odds are, if you're reading this book, you're not one of these people.

SO WHAT'S YOUR MOTIVATION?

The five examples above cover a lot of ground, but they're only really offering the broadest of strokes. Figuring out what's really going on in your head is a highly personal thing, a refinement of those broad strokes that takes time and self-knowledge.

There's rarely a single clear-cut reason writers want to be writers, but there are often layers where one thing is more important than the other. Me, I'm a massive egotist with a healthy side-order of mercenary impulses. I want the audience, and I want a long-term career, and I want to pay my rent.

And yet, within this spectrum, one of the most powerful realisation I ever had about what I really wanted came from an off-hand comment in a review. The reviewer had noted that my short fiction was popping up everywhere that year, and the frisson of recognition when I read through that was eye-opening. Being thought of as *prolific* brought me a kind of satisfaction, far more so than any of the individual publications did on their own. It immediately coloured my long-term thinking and shifted my approach to new work.

So how about you? What do you really mean when you say, "*I want to be published?*" What do you want to get out of writing that being published will get you closer to?

2018 COMMENTARY

I wrote this after a really frustrating day answering questions at my writers centre gig, and I was really nervous about putting it out because it flew in the face of so much advice you get as an aspiring writer. It quickly became one of the most read posts on my website, courtesy of the agents and editors who started sharing it around.

Two interesting things that I've noticed, after talking about this post for a few years.

First, the assumption that five books equals a steady following comes with a bunch of assumptions about who you're publishing with (mid-to-large traditional publishers) and what you're writing (sticking to the same genre). If you're working with small press, or going indie/self-publishing, it's best to take the spirit of the advice rather than the exact number.

Second, people's reluctance to identify their own values with regards to their writing can result in a particularly frustrating form of mission drift.

When we start out, our practice will often revolve around writing the absolute best story or novel we can produce. Writing isn't earning our rent money and there's no deadlines, so we can take the time to work and rework everything. There's a corresponding shift towards focusing on the craft, working at the limits of our ability and stretching our practice in new directions. This stretching and learning is part of the pleasure of writing, which can make up for the fact that it takes a lot longer for the money to start flowing in.

It's much harder to keep working at the limits of your skill set when you're a full-time writer relying on freelance income. Freelancers don't get paycheques, they get payments for work that's finished. Your ability to pay rent is predicated on delivering fast, on-time, and competently.

Some people are okay with competence, but others miss that feeling of working at their limits. They want to recapture the feeling of being an artist, not a craftsman. They find themselves frustrated by the feeling that there's too little time, too many deadlines, and too little money to buy themselves a break in the schedule.

They want the income of being a working writer, but it doesn't serve their creative values they're applying to their work. Even when they write something competent and publishable, they resent the fact that it's not the absolute best they can do.

Working out of sync with your values gets frustrating, which means decisions need to be made. Do you cut back on work to give each project more time? Do you quit freelancing full-tie and get a part-time job to pay the rent? Do you accept that earning rent means more right now, and set aside your concerns to address at a later date?

There's no right or wrong answer here, because every writer values different aspects of their career in different ways. It's one of the reasons giving advice is so hard right now: writing careers are a sequence of decisions, and most days you have to throw your weight behind one particular desire at the cost of others.

Being conscious of what you value about your work helps decide what can be sacrificed, when the time comes, and what you need to fight for with everything you've got.

---

1. Well, almost no way. Publishers will, of course, come around *fast* if your blog has a huge audience they can leverage to sell books.
2. This is one of those signs that suggests indie publishers and traditional publishing are working very different business models.
3. Alternatively, a YouTube channel, Facebook Page, or Podcast.

Focus On the Mountain, Not the Map

ORIGINALLY POSTED NOVEMBER 10, 2015

So Neil Gaiman has this speech, a keynote address he delivered in 2012. You may be familiar with it — almost everyone is, at this stage of the internet, 'cause that shit has been linked to and reprinted more times than the goddamn Bible.[1] Peeps will repeat the words *Make Good Art* like a goddamn mantra.

I don't mind that. As mantras go, *make good art* is pretty bloody aces.

But for my money, the most valuable part of the speech isn't the bits that get repeated over and over. It's not in the catchy phrases about making good art when your cat dies or your wife leaves you. It's not in the sequence where he lays out his beliefs that there are no rules in art, which creative types lap up like the fun-loving anarchist spirits we all dreamt of becoming when we first decided to pursue a career as an artist.

The most valuable part of the speech revolves around the metaphor Gaiman used to guide his career as a young writer. He pictured his long-term goal — being a working author who wrote good stories — as a distant mountain he needed to reach. This was an important, because:

> *...I knew that as long as I kept walking towards the mountain I would be all right. And when I truly was not sure what to do, I could stop, and think about whether it was taking me towards or away from the mountain.* (Neil Gaiman, *Make Good Art*)

I mean, holy shit. That is genius. Seriously, fucking brilliant.

For Gaiman, this metaphor became a way of evaluating opportunities. He said no to certain editorial jobs he was offered, because they were a backwards step for where was at the time. They weren't bad jobs, and they would have moved him closer to the mountain if they'd come along earlier, but now they represented a step further away.

Therein lies the genius of Gaiman's metaphor: it places opportunities in a long-term context, with an end-goal in mind. Exactly the kind of thing most writers need to remember — and often suck at recognising — rendered into a simple image that's easy to understand.

Figure out your mountain, and focus on moving towards it.

I want to focus on the flip side of this, which is just as important, because there is a long tradition of aspiring writers doing just the opposite. Instead of figuring out the mountain and moving towards it, they do something else.

ASPIRING WRITERS MAP SUCCESS ONTO WEIRD-ASS SHIT AND REFUSE TO LET IT GO

Ask any established writer or editor, and they will tell you war stories about the time they stood between a new writer-type and a "big break". We share these stories with other professionals, show them off like battle scars when we're getting drunk at conventions. We all have them.

All of us.

And it's not like the new writers in these stories set out to be crazy as a bucket of weasels soaked in gasoline and playing with matches. It's just ... well.

Writing, it's not a career with established *roads*, is it?

It's not like you show up, fresh-faced and eager to be a writer, and people start giving you clear instructions the same way they would if you said things like lawyer or doctor or taxi driver. People know how to get those jobs. They understand the paths you need to take, in a general sense, even if they have never followed those paths themselves.

But writing? Say those fateful words, 'I wanna be a writer,' and you'll be greeted with a chorus of 'there's no money in writing,' followed by the much-loved coda of 'artists only get famous after death.' And even if you're a bright and precocious type, pointing out all the writers who do seem to be having careers, people will tell you it's a one in a million chance.

The message basically boils down to this: Successful writers are *aberrations*, kid. They are super-special snowflakes touched by the bright spark of genius. How dare you assume you are one of them? Their path is not your path.

And it doesn't take long to figure it out: no-one seems

to have any fucking idea about how to get to the mountain, which means you've got to figure out for yourself.

And so new writers get *ideas* about the way things work. They're lost in the wilderness without compass or road signs, and they sketch out maps in the dirt based on what they know.

Some of those maps are pretty good. If you've done the research, gotten the lay of the land, figured out where other people have taken the wrong path and wandered into terrain that should be marked with stuff like *HERE BE FUCKING DRAGONS*. The writers in question know that it's a bad, bad idea to wander into the terrain where the dragons will eat you. They are aware of the things to avoid and the options available and how to leverage their skills to get to where they're going.

Not all maps are like that.

Frequently, there are maps that are full of sketchy details. Crude scrawls that depict a hell, a forest, and a little trail of dashes. Maybe a little stick figure sitting atop the lonely mountain of success, preparing to dive into an ocean of money like he's Scrooge McDuck.

These folks want success, but they don't really know how to get there, and when they find something that resembles one of their sketchy details, they cling to it with both hands.

Those sketchy maps will take people down all manner of treacherous roads, full of dead ends and wolves and scary-as-shit forests where people get lost, and because the map is bad and the mountain seems so far away, people get lost.

Or they mistake the map for the destination.

This is the point where bad decisions get made. It's the place where aspiring writers will pay obscene amounts of money to vanity publishers, because they have mapped "success" onto "having a book."

It's where aspiring writers will self-publish with no particular plan, because they have mapped "success" onto "getting your work out there," regardless of the challenges associated with being your own publisher.

It's where aspiring writers who haven't researched the road at all will scream abuse at established writers who refuse to read their work, or slip manuscripts under toilet doors while an editor is trying to pee, because they have mapped "success" onto "getting discovered".

It's where otherwise sensible writers will say yes to sub-par deals or opportunities, because they have mapped "success" onto "getting asked to write".

It's where writers who get their first book published start assuming the world is all candy and unicorns, because they have mapped "long-term success" onto "getting one book published".

It's where writers think, "shit, if I've just won this award/got this particular break/just scored a review at …"

Well, you get the picture.

Everyone does this — new writers, established writers, it doesn't matter — we've all got this idea of success in our heads and a map, crude though it may be, designed to get us there. We all have some idea of what the mountain looks like, and sometimes it's hard to see it in the distance because there's mist or rain or you're lost in a valley.

This happens. To *everyone*.

And as long as you take a moment to pause and reorient yourself, looking back towards the mountain instead of the map in your hand, there's a good chance you'll be okay. You noticed the map is leading you off-course and start to make corrections. You start moving towards the mountain again. You focus on the destination, not the journey.

Most people don't do that. They get focused on the map, or they keep listening to the drone of their internal GPS, even after people have pointed out the damn thing is probably broken.

NOTHING WILL FUCK YOUR WRITING CAREER UP LIKE MISTAKING THE MAP FOR THE MOUNTAIN

Alright, here is your warning. The moment you map success onto a specific opportunity — pitching to an editor; attending a workshop; meeting a famous writer; *getting you first goddamn book published* — you are primed to lose sight of where you really want to go.

Don't do this.

Ignore the map.

Lift your eyes off the map and focus on the mountain. If you can't see it, figure out what you need to do to get to the place where you can.

And then, once it's in sight, put all your effort into getting there. Pay attention to the paths that will take your forward and ignore the ones which will take you back.

Focus on success, not the map you've built to get you there.

Ask yourself two important questions:

1. WHAT HAVE I MAPPED SUCCESS ONTO RIGHT NOW?
2. IS THAT STILL WORKING FOR ME AND GETTING ME CLOSER TO THE MOUNTAIN?

If the answer to that second question is yes, go forth and do what you do. If not, it's time to take a moment and regroup. Look towards the mountain. Figure out some alternate paths.

And then, to paraphrase The Ramones: Hey-Ho, motherfucker. Let's go.

The mountain awaits.

2018 COMMENTARY

I wrote this around the time of the 2015 GenreCon, both as an admonishment to myself and some general advice to the writers coming to the convention.

There is a very important, unsaid thing at the heart of this post: since so much of our culture tells us that making a living as a writer is only possible if you're a genius, there is a subset of aspiring writers who are convinced that they must be a genius and everyone else is just blocking their access to publishers who'll make their dreams come true.

These folks are generally a nightmare to deal with, and don't do themselves any favours. Some are focused to the point of rudeness, while others are simply assholes no-one is really eager to help

Significantly more heartbreaking are the writers who hear the same rhetoric and choose, instead, to over-invest in the opportunity in front of them. They will run themselves ragged preparing for a pitching session with an editor, or submitting an application to a mentorship program, because they can't see any other way to get access to the industry.

Here's the thing about GenreCon: the editors are generally there all weekend. They're eating lunch beside you, engaging in conversations. They're on panels, talking about writing.

They're around for three whole days, instead of the two hours set aside to take pitches, which means there were multiple opportunities to meet them and talk.

People focused on the pitching opportunity like it was life and death, and we got a lot of static when folks missed out on a shot. I kept trying to talk about the alternatives, but the focus stayed on the pitching sessions. In this instance, the pitch was map, but connecting with the editor in question was often the destination people really wanted. Focusing on the map often meant forgoing the other opportunities to forge a connection, even when we specifically offered to make introductions.

Here's the important thing to remember about any moment that looks like your big break: there are few opportunities are so big and important that they will make or destroy your career. Writing careers build up over time, slowly and steadily, far more often than people are discovered and catapulted to overnight success.

Your career doesn't rest on one opportunity, or the sales of a single book. They may be important steps, but they're ultimately just one step on a long journey.

If you're just starting out, take heart: there's significantly more ways into the publishing industry than there appears right now, and repeated engagement will do more for your career than getting this one thing right.

---

1. You can still see Neil Gaiman's Commencement Address here at time of writing: https://www.uarts.edu/neil-gaiman-keynote-address-2012

Writing, Budgeting, and Shame

ORIGINALLY POSTED OCTOBER 19, 2010

My primary activity at the moment is *not* doing things, which is not conducive to exciting bloggery. For example, I'm *not* succumbing to the temptation to renew my Locus subscription; I'm *not* rushing out to buy the passel of books I really want to buy; I'm *not* going on online shopping sprees to celebrating the moment of parity between the Australian dollar and the US. In fact, I'm not really leaving the house much for anything, really.

All of this takes considerable mental energy on my part, because the impulse is there to do all of them and in some cases (say, Locus Magazine) I can even partially justify why I *should* do them. Such are the realities of paying off credit card debt in my current circumstances – I've trimmed my budget to focus as much as possible on paying off the accumulated debt of the last year, and even then the realities of credit interest meant I'm only dropping the debt by $5-$20 a month. Eventually that will change – the payments will knock down the debt, the not-using-the-credit-card will keep new debt from accumulating, and thus there will be less interest as the months go by – but that day is a ways off. At the moment the best option available to me is getting used to not doing things, even if it's hard and depressing and largely un-fun.

So the question becomes: why am I blogging about this? Well, call it a lesson in the psychology of being a writer (or, at least, this writer).

Like many people who muddle by in the world, I'm not actually terrible with money. I'm not *great* with it, but my bills get paid and my rent goes in on time and I'm rarely without food. Between post-graduate studies, a tendency towards casual employment, and a focus on writing as a long-term career, I've gotten used to living on the kind of paycheque that hovers around minimum wage. It's frustrating, sure, but it also means I get to do the kind of writing I want to do above all else.

Most days I'm okay with the trade-off: I earn much less now, in favour of putting more time into doing the thing I'm good at, because I know writing is a long game. Success, if it happens, tends to accumulate.

Until about five years ago, I managed to avoid debt trouble by either not having a credit card, or keeping said credit card with a low credit limit and paying the damn thing off within a month of using it.

But, like most people, there were gaps in my budget. Unexpected expenses where I'd leak cash like a sieve, spending without thinking, then shore things up next time I got paid. When I stopped receiving a regular paycheque a few years back, the outlet for those expenses became the credit card and the refilling ceased to happen on a regular schedule.

My first budgeting blind-spot largely came down to purchases justified under the aegis that 'I needed things for writing.' Stuff like printer ink cartridges would get charged to the card on the weeks that I didn't have the ready cash for them, or I'd look at a magazine like Locus and rationalise the subscription. Or I'd celebrate a story sale by hitting the bookstore, working off the theory that I'd pay things back when the cheque came in, even though I'd largely spend that money two or three times before it actually arrived. Yes, this is thoroughly stupid, but I suspect many people are stupid with their credit cards in much the same way because that's how the companies who offer us credit cards prefer us to use them.

And, honestly, it's far less stupid than my second blind-spot. 'Cause my second blind-spot is largely summed up as "shame."

There are hundreds of small purchases on my credit cards that were primarily driven by shame: petrol for the car so I could make it to social events without saying 'sorry, I'm broke'; last-minute grocery shopping for when people where coming around so they weren't exposed to my regular diet of hot-dogs and baked beans; pizza on those nights when the writing seemed hopeless, and therefore I was wasting my life, and the only defence against the lingering spectre of shame was spending money on the simplest of luxuries. Birthday presents I wouldn't have been able to afford under ordinary circumstances. Christmas. Meeting people for coffee.

Simple , ordinary things that I just couldn't bring myself to admit weren't in the budget. It was rarely a lot of money, only ten dollars here and twenty dollars there, but it quickly added up when there wasn't a paycheque to allow for a timely repayment.

And to be fair, this probably wasn't needed — my friends and family have always been pretty good about understanding when I say, 'sorry, the money's not there.' The problem largely came down to me. Doing those things were a way of bolstering my self-esteem rather than taking the hit of saying 'I don't have the cash', and it was a way of warding off the sinking feeling that maybe I just wasn't good enough to do better. For years I warded off that feeling with the excuse of "post-graduate study", but when I left the degree behind I no longer had that defence, and thus the credit card stepped in to pick up the slack.

I may well be alone in this, but I suspect this is the real danger when budgeting as an aspiring writer without a full-time day job: it's hard to keep your eyes on the future and accept that you're doing without now, especially if you've been doing without for a while. Writing is one of those careers that doesn't have immediate payoffs, may never have a payoff at all, and doesn't get a hell of a lot of respect in ordinary society. When you pick writing and you aren't making a success of it, odds are there's going to be a moment of shame somewhere in your future — the culture virtually demands it. You'll feel it in your gut the first time you tell someone 'I'm a writer' and they respond with the handful of usual response that statement gets. It's one of the best reasons I can think of to listen to writing books when they say stuff like 'don't give up your day job.' Hell, it's the reason why I was much more productive when I had a damn day job and I really miss having one. It's much easier to be proud of your work when you're not wishing it'd earned you the discretionary cash to buy a new book, meet a friend for coffee, or afford a McDonald's burger.

I spent a lot of time trying to figure out why I was so interested in blogging this budgeting/credit card process, and it largely came down to the idea of writing without a net (ie, putting my process out there, warts and all) and a desire to just admit to the shame so I could stop worrying about it so much (cause, honestly, I don't see it going away). A writer far smarter and more successful than I (probably John Scalzi) once blogged that writing is a career for people who enjoy being in a constant state of panic. I think that's probably true, but it's a mistake to think that all the panic is going to come from deadlines and late cheques and wondering how you're going to pay your rent next week. Slowly, inevitably, some of that panic's going to come from not moving as fast as you want to be, and some of it's going to come from fear of failure, and some of it's going to come from the thought that 'maybe this is as good as I'm ever going to be.'

And based on my conversations with people who are further along the food chain than I am, I'm not sure that ever goes away. Somehow you have to figure out how to handle it and keep writing anyway.

2018 COMMENTARY

Despite its title, this post is largely about the realities of being freelancer. What I didn't realise at the time, despite having worked freelance and contract gigs for a decade, was exactly how different your thinking around finance and budgeting needs to be when you're on a freelance income.

Fortunately, it's a topic that sees a lot more traction online than it did back in 2010, to the point where I revisited the topic of writing and money in 2016, which includes a series of useful posts by other writers that I update as I find new resources. You can find that link here: http://www.petermball.com/some-thoughts-on-finance-advice-and-writing/

I particularly recommend Kristine Kathryn Rusch's five-part series on T*he Freelance Scramble*, which is one of the most illuminating discussions on the differences between budgeting-for-freelancers and budgeting-for-everyone-else that you're going to come across. And both the money guides

Lets Be Clear: I Know Fuck-All About Writing And Publishing (And That Means I Know A Lot)

ORIGINALLY POSTED NOVEMBER 25, 2015

Every now and then I'll write a blog post that gets a whole bunch of people showing up at my site. This is the drawback of working a gig where you get to know more popular writers, with established fanbases, who occasionally point at you and say, 'yo, this is great.' You start off speaking into the void, then all of a sudden your readership multiplies for the space of a post or two. This makes me very happy, but also extraordinarily nervous.

Because, here's the thing: I know fuck all about writing and publishing.

I mean, I know some stuff, but in terms of the writing and publishing world I am an utter bantamweight. I am thoroughly not ready for prime time. I am three steps into a journey of a billion goddamn steps.

The fact that I have a job where I talk about these things and people listen to me like I'm an expert? Fucking terrifying.

The fact that you're here, paying attention as I blather on? Equally terrifying.

Every instinct I have says shut the fuck up, send people

elsewhere, let them pick this up from people who actually know their shit. When you are trusting me as a reliable source, you are trusting a man who routinely finds himself wearing paper bags as hats instead of putting them in the bin like a sensible person.

The gulf between what I've actually picked up about the topic, over the years, and what I'd need to know in order to actually feel comfortable talking about it? Massive. Immense. Deep as the Marianas Trench.

I know fuck-all about writing and publishing.

I acknowledge that, openly, without any real sense of shame, because knowing you know nothing is an incredible source of strength. It means that you don't take the handful of shit you do know — because we all know a little — and use it to blind yourself to your own limitations. It means you don't assume that just because you've got some knowledge about one particular corner of a field, you're ready to rumble in every aspect of that field.

It means, when you come up against shit you're not sure about, you go looking for resources and good, *diverse* sources of information rather than trusting your untrained gut.

I love knowing fuck all. It means I get to go and figure things out. My blog posts and newsletters are frequently me figuring things out in public, pressure-testing my ideas amongst a group of readers that include, among other things, a whole damn lot of writers who know far more than me. Folks with very different strengths and experiences who will weigh in when I'm acting like a dumb-ass.

Takes a deep breath.

Right.

So…two weeks back, Lifehacker published a really unfortunate article about how to finish and publish your first novel. And when I say unfortunate, I mean *egregiously* bad.

People are going to get themselves ripped by by scam-artists bad.

I hope to god that link no longer works, 'cause in any sane world you'd pull it down due to the potential for shit to go wrong, bad.

People are going to read this and buy into the utterly terrifying belief that spending thousands of dollars at a vanity press will turn you into the next Stephen King levels of bad.

And its the perfect illustration why you need to get comfortable with the fact that you know nothing, 'cause even when people started pointing out the problems with the business model advocated, the author doubled-down with 'no, you don't understand, my situation is *different*.'

Well, yeah. I get you think that, author who we shall name name in order to protect the innocent. But, no. Oh fuck, no. Your situation really isn't.

I'll be clear: it may be that the writer in question wasn't scammed in *this particular instance*. They are, at this point, perfectly happy with their vanity-publishing experience. They may feel great about their decision to fork over large chunks of cash to re-branded vanity press, and there is even the tiniest fucking possibility they will earn that cash back.

Really tiny. Beyond microscopic. No, even smaller than you're thinking right now.

And whether they'll still be happy with their experience in a few years is up in the air, since you can basically mark off the checklist of things you'll get warned about on sites like Writer Beware.[1] This author's article *literally* read like the advocacy pages that appear on vanity publishing scams as they try to convince you they're not vanity publishing.

In fact, it's the kind of article vanity publishing encourages people to write, after their first book comes out, because vanity publishers are usually very clear that the lack of sales are entirely your fault. *The books don't sell because you're not promoting,* they'll tell you. *It has nothing to do with the fact that you're being scammed and there is absolutely no distribution for the three thousand copies we just printed.*

It's made worse, I suspect, because I'm pretty sure the title got rewritten by Lifehacker editorial, which subtly changed the tone of the article by giving it even more authority. And speaking with authority, when you don't have enough to know you're basically talking out of your ass?

Just … no.

Assume you don't know enough. Assume you need to find out more. Make sure you've vetted what you learn and what you think you know against other resources.

When you think you know shit, your opinion is set in stone. You extrapolate big things from very little knowledge. You stop focusing on the mountain and start focusing on the difficulties of the path you're currently following.

Writing is a place where lots of people extrapolate very little into a whole bunch of authority.

Should I ever do that, shoot me.

'Cause I know fuck all about writing and publishing. I can — maybe — hold my own on a handful of topics, with the caveat that I should be one of a diverse range of opinions people study. It's the barest sliver of what I should know, given my current day-job gig and my tendency to write about writing.

I try to be cool with that. I work to fill the gaps. The nice part of my job is that I get to do things like GenreCon, where the program is essentially two days of me testing ideas by putting three or four writers *much smarter and more successful than me* onto panels where they talk out a topic.

I get to sit down with writer and editors and agents and ask questions that fill the gaps in my knowledge.

I get to talk to folks who self-publish and learn what's working for them (and what's not).

And even with all that, it's futile. 'Cause I will never know all I need to know.

That's the nature of actually trying to know stuff — you just become more aware of the gaps.

2018 COMMENTARY

Writing is a complex gig. Publishing — indie or traditional — adds another layer of complexity, which is why there's a whole shonky industry based around offering aspiring writers easy answers to questions like 'how do I get published?'

One of the worst parts of working with writers for so long is the number of people who ask for help after they've gone the vanity publishing route, looking for ways to recoup the thousands of dollars they blew on their print book. 'How do I promote?' they ask, or 'How can I get my book into stores?'

Often, the answer is not to their liking, because most vanity publishers on the shonky end are taking advantage of people's naivety about publishing and utter belief that getting published is synonymous with success. They'll produce five thousand print copies with substandard editing and design, then tell the writers that they're responsible for distribution and finding their readers.

Often, they dodge the accusation of being shonky by going on the offensive, rolling out questions like: are you guest blogging to advertise your book? Are you hitting up bookstores to take copies? Are you entering awards and promoting the fact on social media? Are you trying to get on the program of conventions and festivals? Are you pitching articles to establish your profile as a writer?

What made me so frustrated about the Lifehacker post in question was that it was so obviously a writer trying to do the right thing based upon the advice they were given. Unfortunately, everything they said suggested they were being taken for a ride by an incredibly fucking dodgy vanity outfit masquerading as an "assisted publishing" press.

Identifying vanity publishing is trickier these days, since self-publishing makes use of the same kinds of processes. Indies hire cover designers, and a formatter, and an editor. What tends to separate a self-publisher from a vanity press is the mindset of the people they are hiring, the business plan of the self-publisher, and the quality of the work produced. They invest in the things that will actually move the needle on their sales, rather than throwing money at the wall.

If you're not sure what any of that means and you're thinking of going indie, go check out the link to Writer's Beware and start the education process before you start spending money.

---

1. Writer Beware is a fantastic resource all writers should bookmark: https://www.sfwa.org/other-resources/for-authors/writer-beware/

How To Process Publishing Advice, Part One: Use What Works

ORIGINALLY PUBLISHED NOVEMBER 26, 2015

So, having established that I don't know shit about writing and publishing, I figure it's worth talking about filtering the great swathes of writing advice out there. And, more importantly, how to figure out if a particular bit of advice is actually going to be useful to you. I mean, there is a whole bunch of writing advice out there on the internet, and a lot of it is ... conflicting.

Or authoritative.

Or great advice, that is utterly useless to you, specifically, even if it works for everyone else.

So how do you process good advice when it comes along?

Honestly, I can't tell you, but I can offer you the process I work through when vetting a new technique, approach to publishing, or opportunity that comes my way. And I do this a lot, given my various day-jobs over the years, so my approach to taking things on board is pretty formalised at this point.

It also includes one important rule.

RULE ZERO: ANYTHING THAT STOPS YOU FROM WRITING SHOULD BE IGNORED

Not getting stuff done trumps everything on this list. Period. The core of your job as a writer is getting new work done, and there is always advice that kills your forward momentum stone dead.

Sometimes it's because you got the wrong advice, or the right advice at the wrong time. You fixate on a particular idea and it keeps you from writing, or redrafting, or editing. You stare at the blank page, wanting to open with a line of dialogue, and some asshole's voice is saying, 'don't open a story with dialogue, editors hate it,' in the back of your head, echoing so loud that it cannot be ignored.

Ignore the voice.

Ignore the advice.

Rule zero: anything that keeps you from writing should be ignored.

That trumps everything else on this list.

STEP ONE: ASK YOURSELF 'WHO THE FUCK IS THIS GUY?'

I learned this one from a seminar delivered by Kevin J Anderson when I was just a baby-writer – whenever someone is giving you advice, consider who they are and what their background is. Publication histories, backgrounds outside of writing, their current approach to particular aspects of the craft or business.

There is a surprisingly small correlation between *writers who have done a lot of shit and been successful in their craft*, and *writers who offer a ton of great advice about writing and publishing*. It's worth considering taking a look at someone's publication history before you take their advice on board. Why are they an authority on this? Why are you paying attention to them? If they appear to have published nothing, is there something else that makes them an authority on this particular part of the writing life?

More importantly, are they someone whose career you'd like to emulate?

STEP TWO: WHAT THE FUCK HAVE THEY DONE & HOW ARE THEY DOING IT?

Before you take someone's advice on-board, ask yourself whether you'd actually be interested in replicating this aspect of their career.

This is easy on the craft side of things: taking advice about plotting from writers whose complex and magnificent plots I truly admire? Total no-brainer. Taking advice on author platform and social media from an author who is online so much it makes my teeth hurt? A much harder choice, even if the person offering the advice is great at blogging or tweeting, because my relationship with social media is very different to theirs.

Note that different genres will offer different approaches to building a career. Indie and traditional will require different approaches. Business models impact on the advice you're paying attention to. Consider: a self-published writer putting together a novel series and building an ongoing readership is generally working with a business model that is completely at odds with the needs of a writer producing unconnected, one-off volumes for small press.

This doesn't mean you can't learn valuable things from writers working outside your particular area of publishing, but it's worth considering the way their experience is coloured by what they do.

Writing advice is not one size fits all. It looks that way on the surface, but generally speaking writers have built up habits and techniques that play to particular strengths and weakness, different goals and means of making money. Take this into account before you take something on-board.

STEP THREE: WHAT'S THE ANGLE?

Let's be honest — the vast majority of writing advice offered on the internet largely comes with with a side-order of *please buy my books* in the subtext.[1] That's cool by me. I'm willing to roll with that and consider it the price of admission, especially when I'm under no obligation to actually pay for anything before I get the advice.

On the other hand, if I can't figure out why the advice is being offered — or if it's really closely attached to a service with a high price-tag — I start getting twitchy. I want a lot of corroboration before I take that sort of stuff on-board.

When someone presents themselves as an authority or talks about the one true way to do things, it throws up all manner of red flags for me. It usually means they're selling something, or speaking from a very narrow point of view on the industry.

No-one offers advice without some form of agenda, and figuring out where the advice is coming from and why they're sharing it can often be as illuminating than the advice itself.

STEP FOUR: STRESS-TEST THE HELL OUT OF THINGS

Advice you don't use just exists to make you feel better. There's nothing wrong with that – I have a host of books on my bookshelf who exist as the equivalent of comfort food. I read them when I'm having a bad day, and think *if only I implemented this approach to plotting, everything will be fine.*

Then I put the book down and go back to going what I always do, because my process is pretty set after doing this for 20 years.

I like to try things out sometimes, but mostly I read writing advice to justify things I'm already considering doing or refine existing processes. Its main role is sounding good and provide a placebo effect while I get on with things.

Nothing wrong with that, if you know that going in.

Everything changes the moment I actually attempt to implement a process or idea that's a step away from my usual habits.

Advice you actually use should be taken on-board with the goal of actually doing something better, or faster, or more effectively. I want to make sure I know *why* I'm about to implement a particular piece of advice, and what I'm hoping to achieve by doing so, before I put it into practice. What problems am I trying to solve? What outcomes am I hoping to achieve?

Knowing that means I know what success looks like, and I can gauge whether a technique or habit is paying off and worth keeping. It means I have a way of measuring whether things are actually useful, or just the writing equivalent of a placebo.

2018 COMMENTARY

Most books and blog posts about writing and publishing offer solutions to very particular problems. Many of them make grand promises, particularly when they're attached to something the writer is trying to sell.

Very few of them are good at articulating *why* they're offering this particular solution. The solution is usually offered as as fait accompli, as if the thinking, experience, and privilege that informed the solution doesn't really matter.

I'm a strong believer in working backwards, before I implement something. I like to understand the problem that's being solved, and why it's important.

The publishing industry is rapidly changing and not every writer is following the same business plan, which is a big change from the way things were back when I stared writing in the mid-nineties. I talk about processing writing advice because I strongly believe that thinking critically about the advice we're given is rapidly becoming a core skill every writer needs to develop.

For example, since 2011 there's been a strong rise in both books and blog posts offering advice on writing faster, often with titles promising to help you write 5,000 or 10,000 words a day. This time-frame roughly correlates with the emergence of an indie publishing business model that favours rapid release of new product and ongoing sales of backlist titles.

This is great if you're looking to resolve the particular problem of being a successful indie publisher, but this rapid cycle of production may not be at the centre of your process. Some folks just don't enjoy writing fast, or want to engage with the slower pace of traditional publishing.

In many genres, traditional publishing often uses

opportunities that leverage the prestige associated with the work to drive sales of the book, rather than rapid release schedules. When part of your business model is based on high profile reviews, public appearances at festivals and events, and occasionally teaching courses, writing fast is often a secondary concern.

Writing fast can help authors in traditional publishing, but it isn't necessarily a central skills that drives their success in the same way.

---

1. And this book is no exception. Go check out the Brain Jar Press catalogue at www.brainjarpress.com!

How To Process Writing Advice, Part Two: Diversity Your Sources

ORIGINALLY POSTED NOVEMBER 27, 2015

Another day, another terrifying number of people showing up to read one of my posts. This means I'm still brooding on the whole writing advice thing, moving from point to point like Pac-Man trying to reach a power pellet, extrapolating outward from the acknowledgment that I know fuck-all. And I've realised a few things I should have put in yesterday's post about processing advice, but didn't have the brain-space to consider when I wrote it.

SOMETIMES THE BEST ADVICE ISN'T ACTUALLY ADVICE AT ALL

I have a shelf full of how-to-write books that are chock-full of advice. Many of them are really good and I'd heartily recommend them to folks who are looking to develop writing skills, but they're not the be-all and end-all of figuring this writing thing out.

Advice, by its nature, tends towards the general. It's someone trying to distill their ideas and their process into something pithy and easy to understand, which hides the fact that process and business are actually enormously complicated.

The most useful books in my collection, in terms of learning about writing, aren't actually how-to books at all. They're collections of interviews and biographies and writers talking about their specific process, places where there's no need to be general. Where the assumption is people are interested in *their* work, and therefore they can dig into personal habits, rather than aim the answer at a general pool of rookie writers.

My copy of *The Notebooks of Raymond Chandler* are among the most well-thumbed pages in my book collection. Not much writing advice there, but there's so much that can be learned by looking at Chandler's process up-close, the way he'd think out his glorious metaphors and similes and scrupulously track their usage.

The Art of Neil Gaiman? Fucking awesome book for any creative interested in the fantasy genre, because it's a writer sitting down and responding to questions about how he does what he does over the course of a whole career. There's something similar going on in *The Writers Tale* by Russell T. Davies and Benjamin Cook, which is a meandering tour through Davies thought-processes as he scribed his forth season of *Doctor Who*.

And it's not something that's linked to writers, specifically. I've picked up great advice from writing by reading interviews with artists and pro-wrestlers, film-makers and actors. Some of my most repeated writing advice comes from a conversation with my friend Allan, a carpenter and prop maker, where we went looking for common ground between what he does and what I do.

The single greatest resource I have, so far as editing (and, weirdly, editing poetry) is *The Conversations: Walter Murch and the Art of Editing Film*, where Michael Ondaatje sits down and talks to the guy who edited films like *Apocalypse Now*, *Ghost*, and *The English Patient*. There's nothing how-to about it – they basically just talk about whatever shit they find interesting at the time – and because of that the conversation covers terrain you'd never explore if you were putting together a book of advice aimed at beginners.

ADVICE GLOSSES OVER THE MINUTIA OF CRAFT AND BUSINESS

That's great, when you're starting out, and the minutia is just going to be a distraction. It's less great, as you advance through your career and start to master the basics of writing. After a while, the minutia is what keeps you going. You want to fine-tune your craft and you can't do that with larger, clumsier tools that are designed to cut through great swathes of audience.

We are in a business about ideas and making connections.

If you're serious about writing — hell, about any art — don't limit yourself to advice and how-to. Look further afield and diversify the points where you're getting information. Broaden the scope of your research and look for connections.

Courses and advice aimed at beginner writers are everywhere. Advice for journeyman writers tends to be a lot harder to find, and rarely looks like advice on the surface — you have make the connections for yourself.

Once you get into the habit, it gets easy. I've learned great lessons about writing by researching art, by researching poetry, and by researching pro-wrestling.

I've picked up useful tips by reading academic studies

about the way television works, or watching a documentary about designers and the way they express ideas.

None of these are things anyone would regard as writing advice on the surface, but they've had a profound impact on the way I work.

2018 COMMENTARY

What should be added to this post is this: network like hell with other writers and creatives. Beyond a certain point, the best advice you're going to get will either be a response to a one-on-one question or something that comes up when you start talking writing.

Social media makes this easier than it's been in years. Twitter is great for delivering short moments of insight, and the number of people who talk process in newsletters is rising. People you've never met in person start to become a familiar presence in the feed, and you can become a presence in theirs.

Even if you're shy and living in a place where networking hubs like conferences and conventions are rare, getting on social media and engaging with fellow creative types can be a way to start making connections.

I've lost track of the number of writers I've met and felt like we already knew each other, simply because of social media and a critical mass of mutual friends.

There Is Nothing Surprising About A Writer Getting Rejected (Even J.K. Rowling)

ORIGINALLY POSTED MARCH 30, 2016

THE SET-UP: A TREND IN REPORTING MAKES ME ANGRY

- STAGE ONE: JK Rowling releases some of her rejection letters from the Robert Galbraith books via Twitter.
- STAGE TWO: Bloggers and journalists everywhere write articles and posts about this, because pretty much anything Rowling does is news these days. She's JK-Fucking-Rowling, after all.
- STAGE THREE: Every fucker everywhere starts talking about extraordinary it is that JK-Fucking-Rowling – one of the best-selling novelists of all time – still collects rejection letters.
- STAGE FOUR: I lose my fucking mind and plot a world tour where I can visit every journalist and writer who expressed their

surprise, mainly so I can shake them by the neck while screaming 'NO IT FUCKING ISN'T' until they swear they will never do write this shit again.

THE ARGUMENT: THERE IS NOTHING EXTRAORDINARY ABOUT REJECTION

Not mine. Not yours. Not JK Rowling (particularly not when she's writing as Robert Galbraith and no-one knows that yet).

We want it to be news because, as a culture, we'd like to believe that extraordinary talent will conquer the limitations of producing art in a system dominated by capitalist concerns. Great art will conquer, talent will shine through, the good books will rise to the top of the slush pile and find their way to stores.

It's bullshit. It's part of the same cultural narrative that puts a premium on ideas rather than work, and convinces people that just because they've written something there is, automatically, an audience waiting for it.

The truth is this: publishers are businesses who supply product. While many of the folks involved on the publishing side care deeply about the art and craft of writing, they have employees who need salaries and audiences who expect specific things from their brand. They have limited space for new titles and established authors who are comparatively sure bets.

They have floods of new work coming in — some solicited, much of it not — and very limited time to process it given that *there are all these other books they need to publish.* Acquiring new books is a small part of their job, which also involves a busy cocktail editing and contracts and marketing and distribution.

Good books get rejected *all the time*. It's almost like their quality isn't the only factor that determines whether or not they'll get published.

They get rejected because they are not right for the audience the publisher has cultivated, or because they aren't good in the right way, or because a marketing team sits down and says, *well, it's good, but we aren't sure how we can convince others of that.* If a publisher needs to sell 5,000 copies of a book to break even, and they figure the audience for your book is half that, they'll turn it down no matter how much the editor loves your work.[1]

They get rejected because someone has sent their outstanding Science Fiction Epic to a publisher who specialises in romance, and it's just not what that publisher does. Sure, they may recognise the outstanding literary quality of the work, but publishing it would either mean doing a one-off book that's well outside their branding (thus risking time and money on the venture with little hope of recouping the expense), or establishing a new imprint/line where they can start competing in that space (thus risking time and money with little hope of recouping the expense).

At the end of the day, publishers are businesses who are trying to make a profit. Recouping expenses is a bare minimum requirement for that, so they're big on minimising the risk of it not happening.

And new authors are always risky. Even when they're JK Rowling hiding under a mask.

QUALITY ISN'T THE ONLY THING THAT SELLS

Here is the other problem with the assumption that great writing will rise to the top: your writing is a product in a crowded marketplace.

And, like all products in a capitalist system, it's assessed against the same requirements of supply and demand as any other company considering a new product. It's considered in terms of market niche and marketability and return on fucking investment. It's considered in terms of your existing audience and how much effort it will be to add to that audience.

And sometimes products are sold on merits that are not *quality engineering* or *all natural ingredients*. Sometimes the marketing plan is based on things being cheaper, or more convenient, or more easily produced.

From a marketing perspective there is nothing wrong with those plans. Let's say I'm a hungry person looking to eat some breakfast. On some mornings a quick trip to the local cafe for my organically grown, exquisitely crafted breakfast of avocado on toast with a side of halloumi is the exact fit for my breakfast needs. Some days, I just want some fucking Fruit Loops, you know? Or, if I'm feeling health conscious, I'll go for the bowl of muesli.

You know what I rarely try when I'm looking at breakfast options? New forms of fucking cereal. I mean, there are already all these different types of cereal out there. I already have a bunch that I like. Catching my eye with something new is damn fucking hard, even if I'm generally pro cereal. The new cereal needs to be fucking extraordinary, or it needs to meet a need that my current favourites don't, or it needs a personal recommendation from a friend whose tastes I trust, which goes along the line of *this cereal is fucking incredible, you should try it*, or—

Well, you get that we're not talking about cereal, right?

Sometimes, when considering a new book, the publisher needs to figure out the angle. And finding an angle for a new author is hard.

If Rowling actually submitted her novel under her own

name, I would almost be okay with the surprise over the rejection letters. In literary terms, Rowling is a dominant brand on par with fucking Coke. The angle is ready-made in the words *JK Rowling releases a new book.*

But she didn't do that. She submitted a book under a pseudonym. A good book, by all accounts, but it wasn't attached to a name that made it immediately marketable, which means it got assessed by *how it could be sold* and *where the début author could fit into the marketplace,* and *if I publish this, will it knock fucking Fruit Loops off the shelf and claim their market share. Will people rave about it to their peeps?*

And she did it this way specifically because she didn't want to rely on the ready-made angle. She wanted it to be about the work.

Work gets rejected. Art gets rejected. The surprise is not that it happens, but that we're still perpetuating the fucking myths that feed this mode of journalism.

MY REQUEST: STOP BEING SURPRISED THAT WRITERS ARE REJECTED

Every time we express surprise over the existence of rejection letters, we're telling new authors that none of the things I've just written about matter. That publishing isn't a business with business concerns, and all publishers have equal requirements and space in their lists.

And that's not true.

Publishing is a business. So is running a bookshop, or distributing books, or any of a dozen other jobs involved in getting books to readers. Writers are, for whatever reason, encouraged to be the only people involved in the process who wilfully pretend that it's not. Start looking at your work with a publishers eye, as well as your own artistic bent.

And any time you come across a journalist who relies on *isn't it surprising that JK Rowling gets rejected*, punch them in the fucking throat for me.

2018 COMMENTARY

When asked to chair a panel about publishing at a conference or festival, I'd often spend the session trying to get publishers and agents to admit that books are products. Very few of them ever did, because admitting books are products sounds cold and cynical. Cold and cynical really isn't the brand you're going for when you're trying to coax new writers into sending in their work, let alone trying to convince readers to buy it.

Here's what you're supposed to think: Fiction is uplifting. Books are magic. Publishing is driven by passion as well as the logic of capitalism, and all publisher want are good stories.

This means you need to pay attention to pick up the things they're not willing to story: they want good stories that are on brand, with a hook to help drive sales. Good stories that will find a readership, and earn back the money put into production.

You know, just like it would be if books were products operating in a capitalist marketplace.

---

1. Small presses, on the other hand, typically have much lower break even numbers. Indie publishers, lower still. It's why a book can be fantastically successful when indie published, but still not be worth a traditional publisher's time.

5 Reasons Rejection Letters Are Actually Awesome

ORIGINALLY PUBLISHED APRIL 9, 2015

Today we're going to talk about something fun: Rejection.

It's been on my mind a bit this week, 'cause I've been finishing short stories and sending them out blind for the first time in … well, shit, about four years. As part of this process, I'm getting back into the swing of checking markets, putting together submission lists, tracking submission details, and all that shit. That means, in the very near future, I'm going to start getting all kinds of rejection letters, and I am fucking PSYCHED.

And, yeah. Yeah, I know, writers aren't supposed to be excited by rejection. A lot of writer-types love the *Sturm und Drang* that comes when a rejection letter rolls in. They talk about how much it hurts or stings or how disappointed they are that an editor said no. They like to mourn the lost opportunity. They like to … shit, I don't know, it never made much sense to me. I'm a writer. I get rejected. It's part of the job.

So instead let's talk about the reasons having a short story rejected is actually TOTALLY FUCKING AWESOME.

ONE: A MARKET THAT WAS OTHERWISE CLOSED TO YOU IS NOW OPEN

Most short-story markets that are worth getting your work will only consider one story submission from you at a time. This means, once you've submitted a story there, you don't get to submit another one until they say yay or nay to your current submission.

A rejection means that an exciting new goddamn business opportunity has just opened up, because an editor that wasn't open to reading your next story is suddenly willing to consider it for their next issue.

This is fucking awesome.

Now, one thing that I'll grant, this feels less awesome when you're at the beginning of your short story writing phase and you've only go one or two short stories doing the rounds. But if you're a writer who produces a lot and has, say, eight or ten or twenty stories ready to send out, you start edging toward the situation where you've got more stories ready to go than there are good markets, especially since there are damn fine places to be published that can take a really long time to get back to you.

When you've got a lot of work ready to submit, rejection isn't a bad thing— it's a chance to get the next story into circulation.

TWO: A STORY THAT WAS IN THE WRONG PLACE CAN NOW GO TO THE RIGHT PLACE

Stories get rejected for all sorts of reasons that have nothing to do with their quality. Sometimes it's 'cause the editor has just bought a run of stories with a similar theme. Sometimes it's 'cause they don't think the story will be a good fit with their readers. Sometimes, lets be honest, the story just wasn't to their taste.

Regardless of what's written on the rejection letter itself, a story rejection is basically the acknowledgment that, hey, buddy, you submitted the wrong kind of story. You have sent us a square peg, and we are a round hole.

That rejection means you can no go searching for the market your story actually fits, rather than sitting in the slush pile of a market it didn't belong. More importantly, the market that was otherwise closed to you is now open, so *you get another shot of submitting the right kind of story to the editor who just said no*.

This isn't bad news. It's fucking glorious voodoo.

THREE: THIS IS YOUR GODDAMN JOB NOW AND YOU ARE GODDAMN ROCKING IT

Writers get rejected a lot. I knew that going in. My job isn't to rail against the rejections, but to focus on the things that are actually important to my half of the writer/publisher equation. I produce the best work I can and put it in front of editors who may be interested in buying it. If they say no, I put it in front of a different editor. That's my job as a writer. As you may note, it's very low in certainty. It's very high on hearing the word "no."

Measuring success by the number of publications you rack up always struck me as a mugs game, because I've got no control over the editors saying yes. I do have control over how much I write and submit. Therefore, measuring success by the number of submissions made is entirely up to me, and every rejection letter offers the opportunity for some forward momentum.

FOUR: IN THE WORST CASE SCENARIO, YOU'VE JUST BEEN SAVED FROM LOOKING LIKE AN ARSE

I've been pretty fortunate in that I've sold the vast majority of the stories I've written. The handful of stories that haven't sold – and let me be clear, we're talking stories that have been rejected by 30+ editors, at least – well, let's just say there are reasons people kept saying no, and in retrospect I'm pretty thankful to said editors 'cause they've kept me from putting out work that wasn't ready for prime time.

These weren't necessarily *bad* stories, necessarily, but they were definitely … lacklustre.

I can handle bad. Bad is the risk that inevitably comes from trying to do something beyond your abilities. Bad is the sibling of ambition, in many respects; there is often the nugget of something interesting in the heart of every truly bad story.

But the lacklustre ones? The dull ones? The ones you look at and go, *well, I wish that were better*, sometimes you're just glad enough people said no to keep those stories from going out.

FIVE: 'CAUSE, ONE DAY, YOU'LL SHOW THEM ALL

I thrive on being told no. My best writing has usually come out of me trying to prove a point. The more I hear *no, this isn't our kind of thing*, the more invested I become in proving that, *well, just this once, maybe it is*.

Accept my stories enough and I get … well, kind of lazy. Reject me enough times and I'll up my game and come out swinging.

2018 COMMENTARY

I never really experienced much angst about rejection, but I recognise that my early experiences with submitting work aren't normal. Technically, I started submitting stories when I was seventeen, but I had very little input into the process. I'd just started writing, and my dad wanted to be supportive, and he showed his support by handling all the submissions on my behalf.

This had two upsides. First, my dad covered all the postage costs, which wasn't an insignificant consideration in the days before email submissions were common and the price of sending hardcopy submissions outside of Australia added up real quick.

Second, I rarely knew when my work was getting rejected, because I rarely knew when and where my submissions were going in the first place.

It also meant that my work went out with a real shotgun approach, with my dad hitting every market he could find that seemed even remotely accepting of new work. His knowledge of how to submit - and mine, it should be said - was very much a work in progress.

This proved interesting a few years later, when I finally started handling things myself and read through the rejection letters. There was evidence of sci-fi stories being sent to romance markets, or novellas sent to short story markets that didn't look at works over 5,000 words.

Looking at all those responses was a quick crash-course I the things that go wrong with a scattershot approach to submitting, but it took place away from the cycle of anticipation and angst that seems to accompany many people's first submission experiences. After all, I'd been rejected dozens of time before I ever thought about where a story should go, and adding another to the pile didn't seem like a big deal.

Yes, You Are Wasting Your Time As A Writer

ORIGINALLY PUBLISHED NOVEMBER 24, 2015

Occasionally I get this request, either sent through to my email or from someone I just met:

> Hey, can you take a look at my story/book and tell me if I'm wasting my time as a writer?

And, man, my heart aches every time I see that. I remember that stage of my career so fucking well, and it was hard as hell. The fumbling around, the feeling of futility. The general feeling that you have committed to this thing that is a huge mistake.

I made the decision to become a writer when I was fifteen. I'd *thought* about it earlier, but fifteen marked the point I stuck with it and start producing work. I stuck with it long past the point where it was sane, living on the kind of money that made my parents wince well into my late twenties. I took bad jobs because it meant I could work very little and write a whole lot. I got work published, but I wasn't getting paid anywhere near enough from my writing to make that worthwhile, and the number of times I seriously thought about quitting...

Well, it happened a lot.

There were points where it was a god-damn weekly occurrence. I'd work at stories or poems or novels and I'd peer into the future and I could literally see no way that all the effort would pay off. The uncertainty was terrifying. There were all sorts of piss-poor decisions made 'cause I was literally working blind and trusting that somehow, somewhere, there would be a career for me if I just kept plugging along.

And there were successes. Publications, even. But that didn't help. The sheer amount of crushing shame I felt for devoting all my time and energy to this thing that seemed like a god-damn lottery...

Wait. I'm getting distracted.

My point, oh brothers and sisters of the keyboard: I know your fucking pain. I do.

But I cannot read your work and tell you if you're wasting your time, 'cause I can't actually do that. No-one can. Your current work? It's just a snapshot. A picture of where you are right here, right now, as a writer.

It's got absolutely no bearing of where you end up.

I may read it and go, *well, yes, this sucks*, but that's completely okay. Everyone sucks, at some point. There is this myth that if you're a writer, you have some kind of natural talent. That there will be some spark of genius in the heart of your work that other writers/editors/publishers will look at and go, *well, yes, I can see it in there, if you just keep working...*

Bullshit.

That spark doesn't exist.

For example: I spent my first year at university failing every writing assignment I was given. Repetitively.

Regardless of topic and form. Which culminated in a particularly crushing one-two punch from a lecturer, who gave me a 3/10 for a script assignment and then pointed out *this is derivative, callow slapstick, and not particularly good examples of either*.

No-one who saw my work in that first year was expecting anything from me, as a writer. I was young and I was bad, and I was derivative as all get out. If I'd asked any of those people who were reading my work if, perhaps, I was wasting my time, I expect the answer would have been an dead certain, "fuck yes."

I can still remember the hollow terror in my gut that accompanied every mark that year. I'd always assumed I could be a writer, and now it turned out that I sucked.

I'd like to say that I took that as a reason to up my game, but I did not. I wallowed. I blew off classes and basically hung out with my friends and figured...*well, I'm screwed. That career I thought I could fluke my way into against all odds, it's gone now. Time to figure out plan B.*

But I didn't.

I tried, don't get me wrong, but I screwed up plan B just as impressively as I was screwing up plan A. Sometimes the problem isn't a lack of ability, it's simply being seventeen and anxious and still figuring things out. In the end, I stuck with my writing course because I couldn't think of anything else I really wanted to do and I'd also failed the pre-requisites for 95% of the other majors that appealed to me.

So I kept reading. And I kept writing. And, over time, I got better. Still not as good as I wanted to be, or enough to make it feel like the effort was going to pay off, but good enough to suggest that maybe, one day, it would all come together. By the end of my second year, I'd figured out enough to get pretty good marks. By the end of my third year, I was doing well enough that they started talking about me coming back and doing post-grad work one day.

I started selling work — not a lot, but enough, and moderately regularly. And I still felt like a failure, wondering if I was wasting my time as a writer.

I'm not alone in this. Every writer I know has an equivalent story. As I started to teach writing and mark assignments myself, I'm pretty sure some of those stories are predicated on things I've said. In those stories, the evil prick who used words like *derivative, callow slapstick* is me. Sometimes I've said shit like *dude, you need to learn how to structure a sentence*. Sometimes, I'm the mother-fucker who says, *if I have to read another word of this shit, I will fucking cut you. My vengeance will be swift and terrible. This shit is causing me pain.*

I've been the guy who dug a melon baller into the heart of someone's dreams and gutted it. Never intentionally, but I get grumpy when I read people's work, and I've been careless or clumsy with well-intentioned feedback. My general grumpiness is one of the reasons I so rarely volunteer to critique work, unless it's a favour for an actual, honest-to-god friend who will not take it personally when I go straight for the jugular when it comes to the stories flaws.

But the truth is this: you are wasting your time as a writer. We all are.

Right up until we're not.

If you find yourself wondering which side of the divide you're on, there are far more effective things you can do with your time than asking a grumpy writer (and all writers are grumpy) for feedback.

The list goes like this:

1. **Develop your craft and figure out how to write better.**
2. **Educate yourself on how the publishing/self-publishing industry works.**

What got me over the hump — the terrible, aching wondering — wasn't the quality of my work or the suggestion of promise unfulfilled. The feedback I was getting eventually suggested I had some future in this writing thing, but there were long stretches where that didn't come. Even when it did, good feedback alone wasn't enough to cut through the despair of seeing no future in this industry.

What got me through was actually sitting down and putting together a plan, treating my business like a fucking business, instead of just spitting creative work into the wind and hoping like hell I'd get lucky.

It was thinking: *well, the five book theory, that's a thing I can actually work towards*, and then thinking, *wait, if I need to get five books published, I'm going to need to produce work faster than I am at the moment.* And figuring, even if it was wrong, I'd at least have five books to shop around instead of one.

It was about learning to finish shit and send it out and move on to the next thing, and learning not to sweat it if one story didn't actually take off 'cause, yo, *I have more stories to tell*. The list of novels I'd like to write one day number is well into double-digits. The number of short-stories I need finish is into the triple digits and growing daily.

I haven't made it any way that feels like making it yet, but I'm closer than I was. And the number of times where I feel like quitting is pretty much zero, these days, 'cause I know what I'm doing and what I'm working towards and I very rarely feel lost. I do my best to avoid wasting time. I can see the mountain and keep figuring out ways to get there, and even if I don't ever make it, I feel pretty good about getting to the foothills.

Despair creeps into the places where knowledge runs out.

Most writers develop their craft intentionally and assume that the business side of things will work out. That's the rhetoric, after all: you unleash your genius upon the world and you get discovered. All you need is confirmation that you have genius and everything will be okay.

But that's not how it works.

That's the bad news.

The good news is that the industry knowledge is there, when you start looking, and it gives you the sense of progress that spitting into the dark never will. It gives you a measure of control, if you study it.

Embrace that. Nurture it. Give yourself a plan. Be like a fucking shark and keep moving forward.

It will do more for that feeling of uncertainty than one writer's feedback ever will.

2018 Commentary

There's interesting research on the topic of motivation that suggests focusing on the long-term goal may be what gets you moving on a project initially, but *staying focused* on that long term goal will also kill your motivation after a few days or weeks.

This is because setting a long term goal fires your intentions, but staying focused on those long-term goals can be detrimental to your experience. The rewards are all focused on external motivators, like what you'll get or what you'll achieve.

Once your long-term goals are set, your focus needs to shift on what you're doing and enjoying right now. Focus on the routines and the pleasures of the immediate experience.

Or, to put it another way: the desire to write a novel or have a brilliant writing career may get you to the keyboard initially, but if you're constantly focused on those career goals then it'll get harder and harder to come back. What keeps you interested in writing is focusing on hitting your word count for a day, or nailing a scene, or adding another tick to your writing streak.

The fear that you're wasting your time is based entirely on putting all your focus on what you want, instead of what you're doing. I'm pretty sure the fear never goes away, either, because writing is risky gig with no guarantee of a paycheck.

If you're not taking pleasure or satisfaction in what you're doing everyday, then you're going to find it harder to keep going for as long as a writing career takes.

The First Rule of Write Club

ORIGINALLY PUBLISHED JULY 9, 2014

Five years ago, more or less, I was having coffee with my friend Angela Slatter and listening to her complain about the slow progress she was making on her latest draft. *Shoot*, I said, *there's an easy fix for that. At Clarion Kelly Link mentioned she and Holly Black get together in a coffee shop once a week, then yell at each other write until they run out of words. We could just do something similar and it'd get your work kick-started right quick.*

And since Angela allowed that this idea may have merit, we started meeting up once a week to talk about writing, eat ridiculous amounts of junk food, and write up a storm. Thus began Write Club, possibly the smartest idea I ever ripped off from another, far more successful writer and applied to my own life.

Write Club's evolved a bit over the years. We eat less junk-food these days. We meet up during the daylight hours, instead of the Friday evenings we once favoured. There was a short hiatus in 2011, when we both foolishly worked a full-time schedule for a couple of months. Angela now writes full-time, after starting out as a part-time writer/part-time QWC employee; I now write part-time while working for QWC, after starting out as an unemployed slacker who basically failed to get jobs and wrote things to pay the phone bills.

But the core remains: once a week we meet, drink coffee, talk about writing, then bang out a terrifying number of words on our latest project. After five years, it's responsible for getting quite a bit of stuff done.

It's fucking awesome.

Both Angela and I used to blog about Write Club pretty regularly back in 2009. It was shiny and new back then, and people kept asking about it when we tweeted results or posted things on Facebook. These days, well, the idea is a little tarnished and the vast majority of our friends know what we're talking about, so it doesn't get the blog time it once did.

Today I plan on rectifying that with a list of seven things I've learned because of Write Club.

ONE: WEEKLY WRITING EVENTS ARE A USEFUL "RESET"

I'm doing pretty good with the writing routine these days. I get up at the crack of dawn. I hammer out a couple of thousand words. I punch above my weight. I try not to fall asleep on the train ride into work. I am a fucking writing machine with laser-like focus that's creeping up on a 2k/day average.

But I still have weeks where things go to shit. There are problems at work that distract me. Or the rail company does track work just outside my window and keeps me awake all night. Or there's a deadline which requires rewrites. Or my body, which isn't built for this six-AM-in-the-morning bullshit, just says *fuck it* and demands a few extra hours of sleep for a few days. And so I let things slide for a day or two … possibly even four or five.

Then Write Club comes around and gets me back on track. The moment where I get the breathing space to remember what it is I do and why I love to do it, then re-align the mental cross-hairs on the long-term goal. It makes it easier to slip back into the writing routine when I've fallen out of the habit, and it comes around often enough to make sure I don't slide too far.

Technically it doesn't have to be a Write Club kind of thing; over the last couple of months, my critique group has become a kind of secondary check-in that serves the same purpose, and I know plenty of writers who are doing something similar using the weekly, online writing events we run through Queensland Writers Centre and the Australian Writer's Marketplace. It can be as simple as declaring a #FridayNightWrite on Twitter and dedicating an hour to the task, assuming other people will follow suit.

What matters is having that weekly anchor that *you aren't inclined to skip* that allows you to hit the reset button.

TWO: YOUR PROCESS PROBABLY HAS MORE WASTED TIME IN IT THAN YOU THINK

Here's the thing about write club: the four hours I spend at Angela's place are usually the most productive point in my week. If I'm having the kind of week where I'm routinely hitting 2,000 words over a four-hour block at home, I'll head to Write Club and achieve 3,000 or 4,000 words in the same span of time. There's something about the process that focuses me and puts my writing into high gear, encouraging a little extra production.

What's changed? A lot of little things, bits and pieces that are ingrained parts of my writing habit at home, but aren't applicable at Write Club. At home, for example, I'll get stuck on a bit of writing and pace the room a little, or make myself a cup of coffee. Or I'll spend a minute or two fact-checking something on the internet after writing a scene, rather than plunging onto the next thing. Or I'll just sit there, blinking at the grey light of pre-dawn happening outside my window.

The details probably shift from day-to-day, but what remains is this: there are all sorts of little moments where I waste time when I'm on my own. That goes away when there's another person there, furiously working on their own project, encouraging me to cut short my little pause and get back into the manuscript.

THREE: "NETWORK" IS NOT A DIRTY WORD

I've learned a lot from Angela over five years of write club. The most useful thing, however, has been watching the way Angela networks as a writer, and occasionally benefiting from said network when she's leveraged it on my behalf.

I used to hate the very idea of networking. It brought to mind images of business cards and false smiles, the relentlessly cynical exercise of meetings with people I didn't really like or know how to talk too. It was a thing for extraverts, the people who actually liked going out there and conversing with people. I wrote because I hated that shit. I wanted to spend as little time out in the world as possible.

And while I had several friends who were natural super-connectors, capable of discovering something interesting about nearly everyone they met and developing a firm friendship because of it, I'd never really seen someone who approached networking from a quieter, more introverted place.

Then I spent five years watching Angela do her thing, quietly connecting people with one-another via email or quick catch-ups at conventions, doing small favours for people and helping them out, passing on news of this opportunity or that opening to people who'd be a good fit. It's fucking awe inspiring to watch, and at no point does it come off as a dry or cynical exercise.

Turns out, networking was none of the cynical stuff I assumed. It was mostly helping your friends do cool shit.

FOUR: TALK ABOUT THE FUTURE

It will probably come as no surprise that I have a long-term strategy for my writing. It's moderately detailed, in the short-term, and eminently adaptable based on changes in prospects and opportunities in the long term, but it's there and I know the shape of the career I want to have.

While the chance to sit down and write every week is one of Write Club's major perks, I'd be remiss if I didn't point out how fucking awesome it is to sit down every seven days and discuss the state of your career and your future plans with another writer who *gets it*. Someone who understands that publishing is a step, not an end-point, and thinks of opportunities accordingly.

I refine a lot of my future plans at Write Clubs. I figure out which opportunities are good ones and which are bad by using Angela as a sounding board. I talk through the merits of submitting here, or the drawbacks of saying no when someone writes and asks for a particular thing. I pay attention to the choices Angela makes and figure out the whys and wherefores of each step.

Talking about the future, about where I want to go and what I want to do, helps make it more concrete. And once it's concrete, it's easier to work towards, especially on the cold winter mornings that make up my writing time for the rest of the week.

FIVE: MY PROCESS IS NOT YOUR PROCESS, AND IT SURE AS HELL AIN'T ANGELA'S PROCESS

No two writers work the same way. I already knew this, well before Write Club was a thing, but it's surprisingly how well it's been reinforced after five years of working with someone else in the room every week.

Angela, for instance, likes to talk through her work. She plots out loud, figuring out how things interconnect, and she keeps a lot of little details moving in way I can't even begin to comprehend. She collaborates well, as evidenced by works like *Midnight and Moonshine* which she wrote with Lisa L. Hannett.

Me, I can't do that. Once I've started the story, I want it to rattle around inside my skull until it's about 90% done, and only then am I able to invite other people in to read what I've done or discuss a plot point I haven't been able to figure out. The thought of collaboration makes me break out in a cold sweat. I'm happy to chat about Angela's work in progress, but I tend to lock down the details of my own unless I'm massively, monumentally stuck or about to type "The End."

None of that really matters. What matters is that your process works and you're finishing your damn projects. So long as that happens regularly, you're golden.

SIX: SOMETIMES YOU JUST HAVE TO TAKE A CHANCE ON A WEIRD IDEA

Here's something I don't often say out loud, but: Write Club shouldn't exist.

Sure, Angela and I knew each other well enough to hang out during that initial conversation, but this was still pretty early on in our friendship. I'm pretty damn skittish around people I've just met. Hell, I'm like a cantankerous house-cat, jealously guarding my territory and snarling at anyone who comes close. I don't really invite close friends I've known for decades to come around and hang at my place, let alone people that I've only known for a couple of months and hung out with three or four times.

That I opened my mouth and ventured a suggestion that basically amounted to, well, *let us hang out every week for a couple of years, yeah?* is kind of bizarre and utterly unlike me. If it hadn't been writing-related, it almost certainly wouldn't have happened.

Somewhere in the multi-verse there is a Peter who didn't suggest write club that fateful day back in 2009. Truly, I have to admit, it would suck to be that guy.

SEVEN: SEEK OUT LIKE-MINDED WRITERS

Write Club is mostly Angela and I, but it hasn't always been thus. In the halcyon early days, when we'd Write Club on a Friday night like the word-obsessed freaks we were and Facebook was a new thing, there would occasionally be spare bodies in the room. People who wanted to get in on the Write Club vibe and pound the keyboards, based on our enthusiasm for the weekly meet-up.

Mostly, these people would show up for a couple of

weeks and then quietly disappear. Not because they were weak or uninterested in writing, but because Write Club wasn't for them. They didn't groove on the hours of silence, focused on the clatter of keys. Or they didn't want to set aside the chunk of their week for the sole purpose of writing. They wanted something more social, or less frequent.

That's cool, but it's not what we were doing every Write Club.

I remember going to Kevin J. Anderson workshop a few years back, and one of the most interesting things he talked about was starting a critique group in the early days of his career where one of the conditions of entry was being able to produce three or more rejection letters from professional markets. If you couldn't meet that requirement, he said, you weren't taking writing seriously enough to avoid frustrating him and the other writers who were showing up.

Basically, you just weren't in sync with the group.

Mindsets matter. There's a social element to Write Club that's valuable, but ultimately it's about the work. If the choice is an extra half-hour of chatting or an extra half-hour of writing, we're almost certainly going to take the half-hour of writing time. It comes down to the way we think about writing and the way we think about our careers.

If we weren't the kind of people who'd make that choice, odds are this whole thing would have fallen apart years ago.

2018 COMMENTARY

I bang on about networking an awful lot, particularly when it comes to writers. There's a whole other essay about it, later in this book, because one of the best things you can do as a writer is *find your cohort*.

For those not sure what that means, it means identifying the other writers emerging at the same time as you, then working together to build connections, figure out the industry, and support your respective careers. Mentors ahead of the path can help, and helping those behind you is important, but your cohort are the writers figuring out the publishing industry alongside you and they're often figuring out problems and challenges just as you're getting ready to grapple with yourself.

It's been nine years since we started, and Write Club with Angela Slatter is still the weekly event I use to anchor my writing routine.

Interestingly, it's rarely the most productive day of my week in terms of word-count anymore. I still get a lot done, but writing careers tend to get more complex as you go along. At a certain point, raw word count took a back seat to having access to another smart, focused, and well-networked writer who I could bounce ideas off and talk-through decisions.

One thing doesn't change, though. Write club is still fucking awesome.

The Incredible Sucker-Punch of Success

ORIGINALLY PUBLISHED NOVEMBER 30, 2015

Writers talk about failure a lot. They gather together to talk about the long roads they had to hoe in order to get their books published. They talk about the inevitable rejection letters, which arrive and keep on arriving and do not let up if you are doing your job remotely correctly.

We like the failure, as an audience. If plays to our twisted little perceptions that all artists must be punished for doing what they do. Greatness? Commercial success? All perfectly acceptable as long *as it's causing you pain, you filthy wine-swilling arty-boy. DON'T YOU DARE BE HAPPY OR PROUD OF YOUR WORK, OR WE WILL CUT YOU.*

Sorry. I'm having flashbacks as I write that. Moving along.

People don't want you to make art. They feel threatened by happy artists and immediately move to vilify them for the crime of being arty and well-adjusted at the same time. They get demonised the way artists like … shit, I don't know. Adam Sandler? Stephanie Meyer? Taylor Swift? Do we still demonise Taytay, or has she moved onto the vaguely-respectable older artist phase of her career?

Essentially, we denigrate anyone with the temerity to fuse creative output with commerce without apology, or folks who speak to a broad audience. Anyone where we need to pretend that they aren't creating *art* to make the fact that they're making *money* okay.

Creative-types are good at failure. We've got that part of the gig down. All the advice is out there: steel yourself, chin up, keep marching on. If you let the failure get to you, you weren't really an artist anyway.

Let me take a moment to say: Fuck. That. Shit.

But fucking that shit is a topic for another day. I want to talk about success – I've had a few successes, of late, and it's got me thinking about the relative merits and flaws of *achieving big things*.

When I was twenty, one of my writing lecturers suggested that the biggest thing I was going to struggle with in my career was self-sabotage. *Nah*, I said, *that' won't happen to me*.

Such is the folly of being young and stupid.

When you've been told that failure is inevitable, as you are when you say something like I'm going to make a career in the arts, success becomes a harder thing to handle. You internalise the lessons about failure to the point where success is bewildering.

SUCCESS WILL FUCK YOU UP, IF YOU LET IT

Back when I first started selling short-stories, I handled the rejection letters with aplomb. They'd come in, I'd nod, then the story would go back out. Neat and easy. No muss, no fuss. I expected rejection, which means it was easy to cope with.

The acceptances, though, those I would fret about. I'd re-read the emails multiple times, looking for ways that I may have misinterpreted the words 'we'd like to publish this.'

I still maintain a standing policy of not announcing things I've sold until there are signed contracts, because I distrust every possible gain right up until there is legally binding agreement saying it's locked in place. Contracts are the safety net, the thing I can point to if the story doesn't get published down the line. The contract is a *promise*, yo, but shit goes wrong sometimes.

Rejection will take seconds of my day. Success will occupy hours of my time with the doubting and the wondering and the occasional prodding with a sharp stick to make sure there's not a wolf hidden under that sheep's clothing.

Some days I wonder how much more I could be doing if only I didn't spend so much energy on doubting the things that go right.

Fretting about success isn't uncommon, particularly in writing. Success means you suddenly have to deal with a whole new, different bunch of problems that are unfamiliar and strange. Your work is out there: now people can criticise you; now the pressure is on to replicate success; now you have to figure out the balance between tweeting about your cat and tweeting about your story.

You may get asked to do a reading.

You suddenly need to figure out how to deal with an editor who gives you feedback.

Oh, god, the terror of your first contract.

And, yes, if you're a writer who has never published anything, it sounds like bullshit to be fretting about that stuff. They're great problems to have, after all.

But here's the thing: you've invested time into coping with the problems of not-success. You have processes and support networks and you understand what's going on when people say no. That shit is familiar.

This is not.

We don't train for success. We don't prepare for it. That feeling of *what do I do* now will fuck you up if you let it, as will the fear of being put in that situation.

SUCCESS CAN LEAD TO MONO-FOCUS

Occasionally, I write things that are far more successful than expected. My novella *Horn*, for example, which attracted this bizarre readership right out of the gates and got reviews in placed I never expected to see reviews. Or blog posts like *Yes, You Are Wasting Your Time Writing* or *You Don't Want To Be Published*, where the content strikes a particular nerve and a metric butt-load of new people start linking to the blog and bringing in new readers.

And because the natural response to success – once you get past the lingering fear – is trying to figure out how to replicate the process, I spend an awful lot of time trying to do exactly that. Suddenly I'll devote resources to that task that I don't necessarily have.

For example, I usually have some pretty strict limitations on my blogging time. It gets a few hours over the weekend, much less than that during the week, but every time a post starts getting a monster number of hits, I find myself starting to break my rules. Morning writing sessions are devoted to fine-tuning a post instead of fine-tuning a novel chapter. Evenings are spent brainstorming future topics that might fit into the successful formula.

Similarly, when I first started selling short-stories, I devoted a whole bunch more time to that than I did writing a novel. End result: I have a lot of short story publications, but I still don't have a novel-length work out there some seven years after I started selling fiction.

Writing frequently requires giving a little bit of your attention to a whole bunch of things. Hell, *life* frequently requires that.

And there are certain successes that encourage you to stop doing so and start giving all of your attention to the thing you're doing swell, simply so you don't have to engage with the project that has a significantly higher chance of failure.

SUCCESS REDEFINES SUCCESS

We build our expectations out of past experience. If you've got a friend who is constantly late for things, and they swear that this time it will be different, you are probably expecting them to show up late regardless. Even if you intellectually understand that they mean to live up to their promise, your gut will whisper *no, no, no, they're never on time* and you'll adjust your plans accordingly.

Then, one day, they show up dead on time and you are, like, *amazed*. Then it happens again, and again, until you stop thinking of them as someone who arrives late when you make plans. Then, if they show up late, you find yourself way more pissed than you were back in the days when they showed up late on the regular.

Success is exactly the same. You have this idea in your head about what it looks like — *if I just sell this short story inside of twenty submissions*, for example, or *if I can just sell out the current printing of the book* — and then you get run where things happen faster and better than you're expecting and, lo, your expectations begin to reset. You start selling stories within ten submissions, or run through the print editions of your book inside of a year, and suddenly your gut starts whispering that *this is how it should be all the time.*

Your expectations of success elevate in response to past experience and your gut starts whispering *you know, it was like this last time, surely…*

No. Stupid gut. No cookie for you.

This elevation of expectations is pretty natural, for the most part, because generally you do start achieving more as you develop greater competency in your craft. At the same time, it's also enormously problematic when it comes to the way skills develop, because you'll generally start hitting peaks *occasionally* before you start hitting a particular level *regularly.*

In the arts, where people have all manner of discouragement forced down their throat from the moment they decide to become a creative, it can be catastrophic to suddenly find yourself unable to meet your expectations.

SUCCESS TELLS YOU TO TAKE A BREAK

You do something big, and you want a break. It's a natural impulse for everyone, but particularly for creative types and freelancers who are not known for doing things like *taking holidays* or *work/life balance.* The number of writer-types who feel the pang of guilt because they aren't sitting at keyboard twenty-four seven is staggering.

Really, in an industry where you're only as good as your most recent work, success is the time to double down and do more. Personally, I'm *terrible* at this — pretty much every period of my career where agent/publisher types were asking *so, what are you doing after this,* I've adopted the expression of a blue ghost fleeing from Pac-Man and mumbled something non-committal.

This was not the best of possible responses.

I know, because I've spent six years doing weekly write-clubs with Angela Slatter, who excels at building new successes out of her previous ones simply because she does the goddamn work to make that happen. It's been … educational.

WATCH OUT FOR THE SUCKER-PUNCH

None of this is suggesting that success is a bad thing. Success is fucking awesome. I am in favour of success: for me; for you; for everyone who is trying to be successful at things that are not going to hurt other people.

Success fucking rocks. It just wades in with a couple of sucker-punches, so it pays to scout 'em out and keep your guard up. When you find yourself flagging and in need of a break, or suddenly seized by a need to devote all your time to a particular task, take the moment to sit down and re-adjust your mental cross-hairs so you're actually focused on where you want to be as a writer.

2018 COMMENTARY

The interesting thing about success in writing: no-one is entirely sure what it looks like. The whole industry seems to filled by people who are constantly dealing with imposter syndrome, waiting for someone to come along and tell them it's time to go and get a real job.

This has some curious effects on the way we think about success or failure. I often run workshops that incorporate career planning and goal-setting, and lots of people hesitate do either. Many more pick goals that are implausible, citing their benchmark like *success means I'm a New York Times bestseller who can retire on my own private island.*

If that's your benchmark for success, then failure is largely inevitable. Which, I suspect, is largely the point: if you set an unattainable goal for success, you don't have to worry that you might fail.

On the other hand, it's hard to feel like you've done something successfully. Folks are usually talking Stephen King, J. K. Rowling, and James Patterson levels of money when they write this, the folks whose success is largely an outlier.

Not-failing may sound great, but it also means you can't builds towards your success. You can never say, 'Well, I made some gains today,' or accept that you've worked hard enough to earn some time off. Presumably, even if you do hit those levels of sales, scope creep kicks in the moment the high of success wears off. After all, a crazy number of best-sellers still talk about their fear that someone will come along and tell them to get a real job.

Here's the important thing: no-one is good at defining the parameters of success when they start out. It's a skill that builds up over time, rather than a natural instinct. Usually I get walk people through the process of identifying the variables they're working with: who are they writing for? Where would they like to get published? What are their deadlines and the obstacles they've got to overcome? What opportunities or projects would they like this project to open up?

It takes practice to answer these, and it takes consideration, but the results are worth it. They give you a framework that lets you feel comfortable that you've done exactly what needed to be done, and a means of evaluating what went wrong should you fall short of your goals.

Failing isn't always fun, but it gives you information about how to do better and succeed next time.

Networking Tips for Reclusive, Introverted Writer-Types

ORIGINALLY PUBLISHED JULY 16, 2014

'Thou shalt network,' people used to tell me. 'Connections are how you get ahead in any business.'

And me, I'd ignore them. Hell, I was all, 'fuck that shit.' Networking brought to mind visions of *trading business cards* and *ruthlessly finding people to help you getting ahead* that seemed ... well, exceedingly eighties. Right up there with giant shoulder-pads and Duran Duran. I didn't see a place for it in the arts, and it sure as hell as wasn't playing to my strengths as an introverted chap who dislikes meeting new people.

Then I met my friend Angela Slatter, who is one of those networking dynamos who quietly sets about connecting the world together. She hooked me up with my first publisher, Twelfth Planet Press, after I told her about the weird-ass unicorn novella I'd written that I figured no-one would ever publish. She introduced me to a bunch of other writers, passed on opportunities I otherwise wouldn't have heard about, and generally taught me the value of being a well-networked writer.

'But what you do isn't really networking,' I said once,

fairly early on in our friendship. 'You're just doing favours for people you know.'

'Exactly,' Angela said. 'What in hell do you think networking is?'

And lo, I was schooled, and the scales fell from my eyes.

So, yeah, I learned my lesson, and while I'm still an introverted, reclusive chap who will never be known for his ability to work a room, I've also become a lot better at building up networking and using its powers for good. I am, officially, a convert — there are certain things in writing you just don't hear about or learn without a solid network of peers around you.

So lets talk networking. Specifically, how to network if you're the kind of person who doesn't enjoy leaving the safety of your house.

GET OVER THE TERMINOLOGY HUMP

The biggest point of resistance when I talk to other writers about networking is almost always a problem of terminology. We've trained ourselves to think of networking as something inherently artificial and false, like the only reason we're going out and connecting with people is so we can take advantage of them. This is a particularly hideous thought when you're one of nature's introverts, prizing deeper connections with a handful of people over shallow connections with hundreds.

The truth is that your network is really more organic and natural than that. It's not about names and numbers you can use and abuse, it's about building mutual beneficial relationships with people you like and respect. It's meeting up with friends and getting to know the friends of friends. Or it's getting to know the peeps in your field a little better, one or two at a time, and seeing how you can help one another out.

Truth is, the terminology doesn't matter and if you let yourself get caught up in the feeling that it's all about you, then you're basically doomed to fail. 'Cause here's the real core of building a network: it's not about you and what you get.

It's about what you can do for others. It's about doing favours.

NETWORKING IS ALL ABOUT HELPING OUT YOUR PEEPS

You're not engaging in a cynical exercise, you're looking out for your friends. When you go to a conference or a festival, you're not getting to know people so you can cynically ask them for favours; you're familiarising yourself with their careers and goals so you can pass on useful information and introduce them to people that may be able to help.

And it isn't just big things, like hooking a peep up with a publisher (although, make no mistake, that's pretty awesome if you can do it).

These days, a lot of my networking activities come in the form of giving a colleague a heads up; I'll get emailed details about an upcoming prize about environmental writing that seems a perfect fit for a YA writer who took a course I ran a few weeks back, so I drop them an email; I see a blog post that I think one of my friends would find interesting, so I tweet them a link and suggest they check it out; someone mentions being nervous about networking at an upcoming event, so I send 'em an email that's a somewhat truncated version of this post.

Forget about doing what's best for you; help out your

peeps without any desire or expectation of them returning the favour. Don't make the mistake of thinking big — a thoughtful *hey, I read this thing, and it seemed pertinent to what you do* is all it takes.

ALL HAIL TWITTER

Social media means that we're often connected to more people than we expect, and it's easy to forget that they're part of your network. I've got plenty of friendships that have largely developed through the exchange of tweets, and many people I've met in passing at conventions that I'd probably forget if it weren't for their names scrolling past on my twitter feed.

Pay attention to your social media, particularly if you're the reclusive type. The occasional reply or re-tweet of those people you'd like to get to know better or keep on your radar goes a long way.

FIND YOUR COHORT

Here's one of the weird things I've noticed about writing – people tend to come to prominence in cohorts and small groups. They're the folks who all started going to conventions at the same time, started publishing novels at the same time, and generally face similar kinds of writing problems at around the same point.

When it comes to networking, it's generally easier to start by networking with the folks who are at about the same point in their career as you. For one thing, you're more likely to be able to do them favours; for another, you'll all develop networks naturally as your career progresses, and you can help one-another out with new introductions as things go on.

While it's a truism that the friends you have at the beginning of your writing career are rarely the same friends you have at the end, the cohort of writers developing at the same time as you are a valuable resource.

PLAY TO YOUR STRENGTHS

If you're a quiet, shy introvert who hates crowds, don't force yourself to work the room at a convention or writing event. Play to your strengths as a networker — find someone you can actually have a longer, deeper conversation with and *have a damn conversation*. Pick the other person who's lurking at the back of the room, looking uncomfortable. Or find a newcomer at the convention and offer to introduce them to a few people.

There's no prize when it comes to networking. Handing a business card out to fifty people doesn't mean that you've done a good job, particularly if the connections you've made are so shallow that all fifty of those people toss your card in the bin before the event is over. One or two close connections can be far more important, if the people you talk to are likely to remember you in the aftermath and you're in a position to help them out somehow.

PUSH YOURSELF A LITTLE, THEN GIVE YOURSELF A BREAK

If you truly dread meeting new people — and man, I'm with you there — then don't put pressure on yourself to spend an *entire* event or conference weekend doing something you hate. For one thing, it's going to affect your enjoyment and that won't make you fun to be around. For another thing, if you're a true introvert, that'll burn you out like no-one's business.

Aim to meet one new person or spend time developing your connection with a handful of passing acquaintances — something that pushes you out of your comfort zone — then give yourself a break and hang with the peeps you're comfortable around instead of beating yourself up and pushing to do more.

TIPS FOR BEING THE KIND OF PERSON WHO CAN WORK THE ROOM FROM TIME TO TIME

Even if you do all the things I talked about above, there are still going to be those moments where you find yourself at an event where working the room is kinda the point. There are all sorts of semi-formalised "networking" events in the arts – program launches, opening night parties, pretty much anything where the vibe is all stand-around-and-eat-canapés while dressing a little better than you usually do.

And occasionally, despite your best efforts, you'll find yourself getting a job in the arts where networking is *an expected job skill.* Or, at least, I did.

In that case, here are the quick survival tips for getting through networking events:

INTRODUCE PEOPLE: The easiest survival tactic at an event where networking is *expected* is to play to the events strength – spend the evening introducing people who may not know each other. Obviously this is a tactic that relies heavily on having a network of folks you know there already, but you can fake your way through the evening with the people you're meeting for the first tie.

LOOK FOR PAIRS: This advice comes from Kim Weisul, editor of Inc.com,[1] and it's proven to be a lifesaver.

At an event, look for the people who are hanging out in pairs and introduce yourself to them. Usually this will be two people who know each other, both of whom are feeling a little guilty for hanging out together instead of networking like the event encourages you to do. They'll be grateful you've given them an "out," so to speak, and there's a good chance you'll be left with one of the two when the other peels off to go start networking themselves.

ASK QUESTIONS (AND PREP SOME STANDARD QUESTIONS IN ADVANCE): Just like all the dating advice says – the best way to get someone to like you is to start asking them questions. Well, asking questions and being genuinely interested in the answers, but the questions are the important part. When you know the event beforehand, and you're pretty sure of the kinds of people who will be there, you can usually prep this in advance.

At GenreCon, for example, 'what's your genre?' is a perfectly valid icebreaker; at writing events, asking about people's books or what they're working on serves the same purpose. In almost every event I go time, some variation of 'what are you excited about right now?' will get the job done.

CLOSE WELL: I'll admit that I struggle *badly* with this one, but try to avoid the standard 'nice to have met you' close to a conversation with those you've just met. Even if it has been nice to meet them, it smacks of being polite and generally not all that interested in the person you've been talking too. Try to start closing with style — a handshake and a genuine thanks for giving you some of their time, or a 'cheers, you've been brilliant company' will make you stand out from all the other peeps they've met in the last hour or so.

FINALLY, PENCIL IN YOUR RECOVERY TIME

When I went to World Fantasy in England back in 2013, I was traveling with my sister immediately after. She asked me what I wanted to do the day following the convention.

'Nothing,' I said. 'I'll need to sleep.'

She didn't really believe me at the time, but when the con ended and we were safely ensconced in a London hotel room, I preceded to sleep for about eighteen hours straight, thoroughly dead to the world. You could have tasered me and I wouldn't notice.

Partially this was the result of a couple of late nights, but a lot more came down to the simple fact that conferences drain my energy reserve. They're fun, and I enjoy them immensely, but I need the recovery time in the aftermath.

If you're truly an introvert — as in, someone who recharges their batteries with time alone instead of feeding on other people — be realistic about what face-to-face networking will take out of you and plan accordingly. It's easy to start resenting the process if you find yourself going to work the next day, without adequate recharge time, so pencil some time to recover and do something for yourself.

2018 COMMENTARY

I spent five years running the GenreCon writers conference, and every time I put networking at the heart of the event. Over time, it became something of a mantra for me: Good things happen when writers talk to each other; Better things happen when writers help each other out.

I believe in networking as a central skill for writers, but

it's still one that's poorly understood. It seems antithetical to the idea of being a solitary genius, and it's too closely associated with the idea of being corporate and sleazy.

I felt that too, many years ago. Here's the good news: you get over it.

Networking is hardest when you're starting out, when you don't know anyone and it's hard to overcome the feeling that you're noticeably out of place. Networking gets easier, with time, because the people you've met and connected with start introducing you to other people. They share their networks with you, and you share yours with them.

Interesting side-note: If you truly hate networking and social events, consider that there might be something exacerbating your natural introvert tendencies.

When I first wrote this advice, I hadn't realised I was suffering from chronic sleep apnea that frequently left me exhausted on a day-to-day basis. Leaving it untreated for so long took my general inclination towards introversion and anxiety, turning them both up to eleven.

Social events still exhaust me now that I'm getting the apnea treated, but I bounce back a hell of a lot faster and dread them much, much less.

---

1. Find the original here: https://www.inc.com/kimberly-weisul/how-to-work-a-room-the-only-strategy-you-need.html

How To Get the Most Out Of An SF Con As An (Introverted) Emerging Writer

ORIGINALLY PUBLISHED MARCH 4, 2016

Around this time last week, I suggested rather strongly that if you were a SF type – and particularly an SF writer – you might want to consider registering for the Australian National Science Fiction Convention being held in Brisbane over the Easter long weekend. Some of you, being astute types, may have glanced at the website and wondered to yourself 'why, exactly, is this event full of fans useful to me as a writer? It's basically just people getting together to talk about the books, films, and TV shows they love? How am I going to get something out of that to advance my writing career?'

Peeps, I've got your back.

First, it's important to understand how closely tied the writing and fandom community is in SF. A lot of great SF writers and editors emerged from the fan culture of the fifties, sixties, and seventies to become prominent names in the field.

This means fan events like cons have been a central meeting hub for industry professionals for a couple of decades now, a place to connect with more established writers and build networks that will stand you in good stead.

And yes, I understand. Going to a con is new and scary and not at all like staying at home to write your book in the relatively quiet of your own room. And it's not just as simple as showing up and being welcomed into the fold, because cons have regulars who already know each other and want to catch up.

Worse, if you're going to a con for serious career development as a writer, it often requires a little bit more effort than simply sitting in on panels (although there are usually some mighty fine writing panels available).

So, let's talk how to get the most out of the experience.

ONE: GO IN WITH A PLAN

If you're going to a con for the first time, go in with a plan and a goal to ensure you get what you're looking for at the convention. *I would like to learn more about agents in Australia*, for example. Or *I would like to meet three other emerging writers I can continue talking to after the conference*. Both are good, achievable plans that can guide your interactions throughout the con, both in terms of engaging with the program and talking to your fellow writers.

Your plan will also give you an opening when talking to people, so don't be afraid to share it. People talk, at cons. They ask questions. Often, when people find out you're attending your first con, the natural question is *how are you enjoying it?*

Fine, you say, and for most non-planners the response ends there, putting the burden of continuing the conversation on the other person. But if you add: *although I was hoping to meet some other emerging writers…*

Well, give someone a solid opening like that, in an

environment like a con where networking is basically *what everyone is there to do,* and you'll find yourself collecting advice and introductions like no-ones business.

(Bonus hint: if your goal is *get published,* you're thinking too broad. That's putting all the pressure on the other person to think through your career path and business plan)

TWO: EAVESDROP LIKE A MOTHERFUCKER

I said very little at my first few conventions. I met people, and was introduced to folks by friends, but when the groups gathered in the bar my favourite thing was keeping my mouth shut and listening to the conversations happening around me.

Mostly, I paid attention to what the writers further along the road from me talked about when they got together.

There are things writers never mention in panels and workshops. Mostly, because it's hard to talk about, say, *the difficulties of being published* to a group of people who would give their right arm to sell their first short story. They're not ready to hear it, and you look like an asshole talking about it in a general setting.

But in the bar? Over lunch? When you're hanging with other writers and the audience narrows? Writers will start talking about *the difficulties of getting published* and *the necessity of multiple income streams* and *which promotional things have worked best for them* and *oh hell, this is what tanked my last book (that I had no control over and was helpless to stop).*

Writers will small-talk about the minutia of their jobs, at a con, the way most other folks will talk about their work. And you will learn shit-loads if you just clamp your lips, open your ears, and pay attention.

When you're at a con, eavesdrop like a motherfucker. And try not to be creepy and obvious about it.

THREE: YOUR HOT-ZONES ARE BREAKFAST, LUNCH, DINNER, & BAR

Your optimal points to meet people are during the three meals every day, and at the bar after evening events are finished. This represent the natural points where people tend to break off into smaller groups, and the phrases to deploy are 'would you care to join me?' and 'do you mind if I join you?'

Your optimal targets in this situation are people on their own (naturally) and people in pairs. Not everyone will be open to adding you to their posse — some folks will just be looking for a break, or catching up to do some business — but for the most part, people at cons *feel* like they should be talking to new folks and networking, so they are remarkably open to expanding their circle or adding you to a group.

Better yet, these smaller groups play to the strengths of those of the writing fraternity who are ... well, introverted and better at meeting new people in small gatherings rather than a crowd.

FOUR: THE ONE-TWO INTRODUCTION

Writers, by and large, are an introverted lot. This makes them hard to meet sometimes, 'cause every new person they're introduced to in rapid succession basically stresses them out. Worse, established writers at cons will frequently have a bunch of peeps in attendance, so there is a wealth of less stressful *people they already know* that they are *dying to catch up with*. Holding their attention is hard.

If you're hitting a con to network, this means that it's not a meet once and you're done kind of thing. Give someone a breather after you've first been introduced, so they can process the fact that they've met you, and then follow-up later in the con to have a longer conversation.

FIVE: ICEBREAKERS

I suck at small-talk. In fact, I loathe it. And because I loathe it, I frequently do very badly at thinking on my feet when talking to new folks.

What gets me through those situations is usually having a series of go-to questions. Stuff like 'how are you enjoying the con,' or 'what are you most excited about seeing this weekend,' and ;what is the best thing you've read lately?'

It will feel cheesy, but it opens up avenues of conversation and it's always much easier to talk to people about the things that they're passionate or excited about.

Things that are less effective as ice-breakers than you'd think: 'I've read your work/I really liked your story …'

These put people in the awkward position of talking about themselves, rather than holding on a conversation. The more socially awkward authors among us will say thank-you, and be pleasant, but it's unlikely to lead to a prolonged conversation.

And since I'm down in Melbourne as I post this, hanging with my friend Allan from Type 40[1] who networks the way most people breathes, I asked him for his advice to add to this. He suggested the following:

> *People like to be asked about themselves. If I see someone I'd like to talk to, I engage them in a discussion about something that they're interested in or something about them. Their fandom, their job, the*

child that they've got with them, whatever they're doing.

But, it only works if you're genuinely interested.

SIX: NETWORK WITH THE READERS

You are not at a con to network with writers alone. Readers are there. So many lovely readers. Meet them. Talk to them about what they're interested in. Find out what attracts them to a book or an author. The folks who come to a con are generally the super-passionate folk who talk about their favourite authors and new discoveries, foisting work onto friends.

They are, in the end, even more important than the writers you'll meet.

SEVEN: HAVE A FOLLOW-UP PLAN

Have a think about what you're going to do after the conference to follow up with people. Friending people on Twitter or Facebook can be a great start, but everyone's social media feeds tend to blow up during con season, so you can get lost.

One of the best con follow-ups I've ever seen by a new writer was David Witteveen after last year's GenreCon. He did a series of interviews with people he met on his blog, which gave him a) a reason to ask for people's email addresses; b) something he could offer the people he met, rather than asking them for favors; and c) a thing that made him memorable, to the point where I went and read his 'zine that he handed over in the final moments of the con.

His post-con communication was polite and professional, his emails clearly outlining the purpose of his interviews, the date it would go live, and his thanks for being involved. It's a simple thing, but it made him memorable among all the people I met at GenreCon, and it got a whole bunch of more established authors paying attention to his blog for a time.

Similarly, my friend Allan networks so well at cons (and everywhere else) because he isn't afraid of follow-up. While I will frequently quibble over sending an email for months after a con, he'll have quickly starting talking to and/or hanging out with people he's met.

EIGHT: SOME NOTES FOR THE INTROVERTED/ANXIOUS WRITER TYPES

If you are an introvert or suffer from social anxiety — and I include this because so many of us are, in this writing gig, including me — let's talk about how to handle the gathering of the SF peeps with aplomb, because the narrative in your head is currently playing its third iteration of *why the crap would I want to spend a weekend around two hundred strangers; that sounds like my idea of hell.*

Peeps, I am with you. I loathe parties. I loathe large crowds. I am skittish and weird about meeting new people, outside of some very strict parameters. My first con was spent half-paralysed with indecision as I tried to figure out the unfamiliar social dynamics, and it would have been worse if I wasn't there with friends.

But what I didn't know then, that I know now, is how to manage the natural reticence of a shy introvert in large-scale social situations.

A lot of it comes down to biology — you're processing a lot of information at once, particularly when you combine new people and new locations, so it starts to stress you out. Here's what you do:

Scope out the locations early. Familiarise yourself in the locations where you're going to spend a lot of time, and get to know them a little before they're flooded with people. It will mean that all your processing is the new people, not the new location.

Focus on the one-on-one and two-on-one. You don't have to join large groups, just 'cause they're around. Your goal for the con is a series of interesting conversations with interesting people, not a big wave of parties.

Socially mediated spaces are ace. The dealers room is a great place to meet people, as is the con banquet. If you're at the first con and you're the kind of person who gets twitchy when you don't understand the social etiquette of a situation, sit-down meals where you're expected to talk are something of a blessing. Similarly, the dealer's room gives you a conversational gambit in the form of asking for recommendations, while also allowing a discrete exit when you go back to browsing.

It is fine to hang in your corner of the bar/room, or talk to the handful of peeps you know, while you acclimatise to the setting. If you're not meeting new people at all, however, you're probably wasting the opportunity.

It's okay to take a session off and get some alone time if you need to recharge. You do not have to be on twenty-four-seven. In fact, if you know that things like cons are going to exhaust you, put some recharge time into your plans before you get to the con.

When in doubt, look for me. Let me know that you've read my blog, that you'd like to meet some interesting people, and give you your goal for the con. I'm more than happy to introduce you to folks I know.

2018 COMMENTARY

Another word of advice about conventions and conferences: get thee to a romance writers event.

Yes, even if you don't write romance.

Heck, *especially* if you don't write romance.

I love a good science fiction convention, but even the most writer-friendly of them is usually still a fan event at heart. It's a place where the readers of SF books gather alongside the writers, and that splits your focus. Part of you is there to network and engage in some professional development, and part of you is there as a writer engaging with readers.

The same is true of most literary festivals, who regard readers as their bread and butter. Writers are there to entertain, rather than engage in professional development.

But romance writers conventions are almost entirely writer-focused. They're started by writers, aimed to writers, and have a long tradition of being utterly professional because they're the genre other folks look down on.

I went to my first romance writers conference and was immediately blown away by the fact that everyone at the conference was a writer. All the panels and workshops focused on craft and industry knowledge, all the networking events were packed to the gills with people who wrote (or wanted to write), publishers, and agents.

Not everything romance writers talk about will be immediately applicable to other genres, but a lot is genre-neutral. We all deal with publishers and agents, for example, and we're all looking to build long-term careers.

---

1. Alan's a pop-culture pop maker and friend I first met at conventions. You can check out his website at Type40.com.au

Al Snow's Advice For SF Writers

ORIGINALLY PUBLISHED IN APEX MAGAZINE #40

Unless you're a professional wrestling fan, you've probably never heard of Al Snow. A wrestler who hit the heights of the mid-card in the nineties, he's never been one of the wrestling fraternity that has broken through into the public consciousness the way main event stars like Hulk Hogan and Steve Austin did.

Despite this, Al Snow is a fascinating wrestler from a writer's point of view. He's spent years behind the scenes, training new wrestlers, booking development territories, talking about wrestling and generally holding forth on the state of the industry. Basically, Al Snow is a smart wrestler who's fond of a good rant about the way wrestling works. There are plenty of lessons he tries to teach that are equally useful for an aspiring author.

What follows are five pieces of wrestling advice picked up from Snow's interviews, along with their corresponding lessons for science fiction and fantasy writers.

ONE: PEOPLE DO NOT HAVE A PHYSICAL RELATIONSHIP TO WRESTLING

The most popular televised sports are frequently those that mimic the games we play as children. We run track and field at school, or play football in the back yard, or we learn to swim. When we watch people competing at a professional level, we have muscle memory and experience that allows us to recognise athletes operating at an extraordinary level. We know how good professional athletes are because we know our own limits.

Professional wrestling doesn't have that advantage. How many of us can legitimately claim to have been whipped into the ring ropes, or jumped from the top rope to plant an elbow on a downed opponent? Even the less flashy moves are unfamiliar, since most schoolyard fights don't start with a collar-and-elbow tie-up. At best, we've applied a headlock, or thrown a punch.

Without the physical relationship to make the action meaningful, pro-wrestling needs emotion to bridge the gap. It tells stories from the heart, looking for ways to invoke familiar feelings that make the fans want to see one guy win and one guy lose.

This is the appeal of pro-wrestling: I don't know the physical actions involved, but I understand winning. I understand wanting to get into it with someone I disagree with, or someone who insults me. I understand wanting to be the best, and the desire to get revenge on someone who screwed me or ruined a moment of triumph. The emotional connection gives context to the in-ring action, something I can understand even if I'm blind to the nuances of the physical moves.

This isn't so different from the problems speculative fiction writers face when creating alien worlds, strange futures, or fantasy empires. Unlike mimetic literary fiction, we frequently present our readers with worlds they cannot physically engage with or understand, and the way in which we make these alien experiences comprehensible is through the manipulation of emotion.

Like wrestlers, we look for the familiar–little actions, big emotions, a place for the reader to connect–so there's a sliver of truth amid the fantasy we're presenting.

TWO: THERE ARE NO BAD GIMMICKS

The pageantry of pro-wrestling means there's a constant parade of gimmicks and personalities on display, ranging from the utterly serious to the utterly absurd. The same company that features Kurt Angle or Brock Lesnar, both legitimate wrestlers with impressive amateur or MMA credentials, will also employ wrestlers whose gimmicks range from the stupid to the deeply bizarre.

Even a cursory examination of websites set up to catalogue and archive the worst of these gimmicks, such as Wrestlecrap.com, will reveal a motley assortment of wrestling heavy metal guitarists, leprechauns, and yeti. Many of these gimmicks have failed, and failed badly.

Yet absurdity isn't the kiss of death in pro-wrestling. Take, for example, the perennial World Wrestling Entertainment (WWE) favourite The Undertaker. His gimmick is absurd on multiple levels: an undead mortuary assistant from the old west, seemingly impervious to pain and capable of causing arena-wide blackouts with his supernatural abilities, prone to terrifying opponents with bolts of lightning summoned from the heavens. It's not just the Undertaker's gimmick that's absurd; over the course of his career he's been controlled by a manager using a supernatural urn, risen from the dead after being buried in a casket match, and fought a motley assortment of similarly bizarre opponents including his own half-brother, Kane, whose pyromaniac tendencies verge on the supernatural as well.

It sounds terrible, and on paper it seems like exactly the kind of wrestling excesses that Wrestlecrap is set up to mock, but over the course of his twenty-two-year career, the Undertaker has become one of the most popular wrestlers of all time. As Snow puts it, it's the wrestler's responsibility to make it work.

That the Undertaker character worked is a testament to two of the enduring truths of pro-wrestling—one, a gimmick is at its best when it reflects some aspect of the wrestler's personality. Mark Calloway (who wrestles as The Undertaker) isn't an undead mortuary assistant, but he is a quiet guy with a reputation for being tough. When the Undertaker threatens someone, it's rarely with words; he simply looms, letting his reputation and stoic calm in the face of violence strike fear into his targets. When he takes a pounding then rises, zombie-like, from the mat, he's merely amplifying an aspect of own personality to extreme levels.

Two, wrestling's audience *wants* to suspend their disbelief. What should have been a terrible gimmick works because the wrester behind the gimmick embraced it wholeheartedly, treating even the most absurd elements of his gimmick as though they were entirely plausible and serious. While it would be all-too-easy to treat his character as a joke, or allow others to do the same, The Undertaker endures as a supernatural "phenom" that terrifies even the bravest opponent some two decades after he debuted the character in 1990.

There are two lessons here for writers.

First, even the most absurd ideas can be transformed into something extraordinarily compelling if they're taken seriously and you find a core truth that allows you do so. Readers take their cues from the work itself; a work that treats a seemingly goofy idea with utter seriousness will allow the reader to do the same. The moment you play it for laughs, the reader is free to stop treating it as meaningful.

Second, respect your audience no matter what project you're working on. As your career progresses, you'll be invited to work for anthologies whose topics strike you as bizarre, or writing for a genre that's outside your comfort zone. In these situations it can be easy to play the theme or genre for laughs, but you owe it to the fans to play it straight and deliver the best work you can. They want to suspend their disbelief, and they won't appreciate it if you're the guy who chooses to complain about his gimmick rather than figure out how to make the character work.

THREE: IF EVERYONE ELSE IS TALKING, BE THE GUY WHO'S YELLING

It's a piece of advice Snow inherited from one of his mentors, and it basically translates as do *the opposite thing of everyone else in the company*. It's an easy way for a wrestler to stand out and get noticed. It may not make you friends, but if it works then it can get you over.

The history of pro-wrestling is filled with examples where exactly this approach has worked. In the mid-nineties the WWF was filled with wrestlers using colourful gimmicks aimed primarily at children — wrestling clowns, wrestling garbage men, wrestling minotaurs — and in the middle of it all was a foul-mouthed redneck named Steve Austin who wore black trunks and kicked ass. It's a gimmick that immediately caught on with the crowd, elevating Stone Cold Steve Austin to the top of the wrestling card and beyond.

In more recent years, to the surprise of many wrestling fans, wrestlers like the straight-edge CM Punk and technically oriented Daniel Bryan have risen to the top of the WWE roster. Both performers had long careers on the independent scene, working for smaller promotions, but were frequently regarded as being "non-WWE" wrestlers when they signed for the world's biggest wrestling promotion. Yet their styles and promos were a stark contrast to the rest of the roster, and their talent earned them a following amongst the WWE crowds.

Writers are given the same option. Short story writers submitting to themed anthologies can do worse than to create a list of the most obvious stories suggested by the theme and doing the opposite. Novelists can look toward the number of SF and Fantasy writers who have made their careers by going against the norms of the genre at the time.

FOUR: THE WRESTLING BUSINESS IS ACTUALLY THE WRESTLER'S BUSINESS

There are plenty of people involved in wrestling who never get involved with the in-ring action. Promoters put on the show; bookers schedule the matches and determine the long-term storylines; in the modern television era there are writers putting together words that go into the wrestler's mouths.

None of this matters, Snow argues, once you step into the ring with your opponent. Once there, it's the face's job to get himself over (win the approval of the crowd), while the heel's sole task is to generate heat (make the crowd wish he'll get beaten), and it's up the wrestlers to do the bulk of the work and ultimately pop the crowd. Even when faced with an uncooperative opponent, a wrestler has the freedom to change their tactics in order to generate the heat or approval they're after.

Despite this, some wrestlers have convinced themselves that many of the people that put the show together hold the power in the industry. They lose sight of the fact that the promoter provides the venue, the booker makes the matches, but it's the wrestlers who have to do the work and entertain the crowd one they're given the opportunity.

And without the wrestlers, the business falls apart.

Wrestling, like publishing, requires a level of synchronicity between the creative talent and the team that produces and distributes their respective creative products. Despite the fact that publishing doesn't work unless writers produce books, many writers have adopted a similar mindset to pro-wrestlers, ceding power to their editors and publishers without acknowledging the importance of their own role. The editors suggested changes are treated as law, regardless of the writer's intent. The concept of questioning a contract, let alone negotiating it, seems strangely inconceivable, especially when writing short stories or poetry.

Publishers and editors, like wrestling promoters, provide an opportunity. It's up to the writer to make the most of that and entertain the crowd.

FIVE: THE BEST MATCH EVER?

One of the recurring themes of any Al Snow shoot is that wrestling is a business. It may be fake — it's always been fake — but the wrestler's job is to get in there and put on a match that allows fans to suspend their disbelief and buy into the illusion that it's real. This is no different from fiction, at all, and it's one of the reasons I'm always perplexed when people look down on pro-wrestling.

In Al Snow's wrestling world, "good" is less valuable than "profitable." He looks at Wrestlemania III, arguably the biggest and most-watched wrestling show of all time, and challenges the conventional wisdom of wrestling critics that suggests that the technically brilliant match between Ricky Steamboat and Randy Savage was better than the headline match between Hulk Hogan and Andre the Giant. The critics aren't wrong. You can find both those matches on YouTube if you search, and there's no doubt that watching the athletic display of the former is far more interesting than the plodding action of the latter.

But people paid to see Hulk Hogan — a charismatic bodybuilder with a five-move arsenal — go out and body slam Andre the Giant, and that makes it the best match on the card in Al Snow's world. Hulk-Andre made the company money, it kept people coming back for more, and it had casual fans invested even if the hardcore wrestling fans would rather watch the guys in the mid-card.

Hulk-Andre elevated the wrestling industry. It made the WWF (now the WWE) more money, which filtered down to everyone working on the lower card, and allowed many more wrestlers to have a career.

Given the choice of being Ricky Steamboat or Hulk Hogan, I'd still probably choose to be Steamboat. He was smaller, faster, more athletic, and over the course of his career, he drew plenty of money as a wrestler. People paid to see him wrestle, to see him gain and defend championship belts, to see him face-down nemesis after nemesis. He coupled quality matches with the ability to make money, and while he never became the star Hulk Hogan did, you'd be hard pressed to say that he didn't do okay for himself.

But it's stupid to look down on Hulk Hogan when what he's doing works. When what he's doing is bringing other people to the show, and creating the platform that allows everyone else to earn money as well.

Replace "Hulk-Andre" with *Twilight* and you're probably seeing the analogy I'm making. I may not enjoy *Twilight* as a reader — I find it enormously problematic as a cultural phenomenon — but that doesn't mean I want it to cease existing. By some objective standards it may qualify as the best book in publishing history — it's not only a blockbuster that generated new readers, but it's now spawned a second blockbuster (equally maligned) in the form of *50 Shades of Grey*, and that income allows their respective publishers to produce works by other writers.

Wrestling may be fake, but that's why I find it interesting. These five pieces of advice have been culled from hours of Al Snow's discussions, and it barely touches on the narrative complexities specific to the kind of storytelling that pro-wrestling does on a day-to-day basis.

As a storyteller, I'm always eager to learn more about the narratives I consume, regardless of whether they're film, fiction, television, or pro-wrestling. At best, I learn something that informs my own practice. At worst, I get to watch smart, passionate people talk about their creative process in interesting ways. In this respect, Al Snow is a goldmine, as smart and passionate about pro-wrestling as any SF author is when asked to talk about their art.

REFERENCES & RECOMMENDED VIEWING

Guest Booker with Al Snow: The Attitude Era, Kayfabe Commentaries

Secrets of the Ring with Al Snow, Ring of Honor

Shoot with Al Snow 2008, RF Video

2018 COMMENTARY

I wrote a slightly different version of this essay for my blog in 2012, but Lynne Thomas (then Editor of *Apex Magazine*, now one of the brains behind *Uncanny Magazine*) got in touch to ask whether I'd be interested in transforming it into an article.

SF Editors who are wrestling fans are a wonderful thing, and there's more of them than you'd expect.

Obviously I said yes, condensed things down to an essay, and discovered the joy of claiming wrestling DVDs as a tax deduction that year.

The lesson here isn't that writing is a gig full of pretty weird deductions, but that writing is a gig where you can leverage the same work in slightly different and unexpected ways.

This is the thing that's often overlooked when people say there's no money in writing. The payment for an individual story may not be great - usually in the region of 5c a word - but if you resell that story over and over across the length of a twenty year career it can start adding up.

Blogging may be something you do for free, but every now and then you'll write something that someone wants to reprint and you'll pick up some quick and unexpected cash.

The trick is getting enough things out there, earning money in unexpected ways, that it starts to add up. Often this takes time and more books than people think, but it's worth keeping in mind as you figure this writing thing out.

Patreon, Tools, Tactics, and Strategy

ORIGINALLY PUBLISHED DECEMBER 7, 2017

Patreon announced a change in its fee structure in December of 2017, which prompted an outpouring of tweets from a number of writers I follow who both use the platform and wanted to talk about the negative consequences of the change.

The changes didn't last long. The new fee structure was dropped within 48 hours of going live, largely thanks to the response from creators and patrons who used the service who were extremely vocal in their displeasure.

Patreon, I'm sure, would like to forget their mistake and move on to the next solution, but I'd like to take a moment to explore how they fucked up before we discuss why it's interesting.

HOW PATREON GOT THE CREATIVES & FANS OFFSIDE

The initial framing of the announcement suggested the change was a good thing for the creators using Patreon, ensuring they will take home exactly 95% of every pledge instead of losing a chunk to fees.

Unfortunately, it did so by pushing the processing fee onto the patron and this had subtle knock-on effects for the assumptions surrounding the service.

For starters, a lot of creators using patreon relied on $1 pledges as their bread and butter. Those pledges started going away the moment this change was announced, because passing the fee on to the pledger means a series of $1 pledges every month actually ends up costing a buck thirty-seven or so. Multiply that out over a year, and you're looking at an extra $4.44 a year to kick a little change to the creators you patronised. This might not seem like a lot, but for a platform that is built itself on the concept of huge numbers of people making micro-transactions, that's a pretty big shift.

This resulted in a couple of general themes and concerns that ran through online discussion. First, that this was a move to drive away the small, consistent donors and make supporting creators at higher rates more appealing.

The second major topic was how the fee would be applied to people who are supporting multiple creators, which Patreon has traditionally bundled into a single charge to minimise fees. If you supported 8 creators at a buck a piece, the original fee was charged on an $8 pledge every month instead of 8 individual $1 pledges. Now each $1 pledge would attract its own fee, with each getting passed on to the person pledging support.

Unsurprisingly, the third major topic was *what are the other options*, with a recurring theme of people setting up PayPal buttons in response to the news or exploring similar platforms being developed by the team at Kickstarter.

Few got much traction, because Patreon got the message they'd fucked up pretty early. They backed away from the change and promised to talk to creators about better ways to achieve their stated goals. At time of writing, Patreon operated under its old system, but I doubt anyone believes that system will stay.

Because the message being sent to the creatives using the platform is clear: Change is coming. The tool is evolving whether you like it or not, and the folks in charge are not you.

Smart creators are already putting some serious thought onto how they can insulate themselves, should they dislike the new approach Patreon settles upon.

NOW, LET'S TALK ABOUT WHY THIS WAS INTERESTING

I'm intrigued by Patreon, but I have no real skin in the game. I looked at the possibility of setting one up earlier this year, for a very particular fiction project, then figured there were ways to monetise what I wanted to create that better suited my circumstances.

What intrigues me about this is that I've seen this process before with other digital tools. When it comes to monetising creative work on the internet, this *Sturm und Drang* kicks in as the tools mature and change, and the tactics associated with those tools are forced to mature along with them.

I watched it happen in the gaming industry around 2005, when the platform that made digitally publishing RPG books changed the fees it charged for the first time.

Another round of changes followed soon after, when a viable contender to the reigning heavyweight platform emerged, and they changed policies to secure their business (and encourage people to stay exclusive to their store).

A third round of changes began when the vendor

sought to move smaller presses with a handful of products out of a crowded marketplace, hoping to make digital books ales more appealing to major players.

Keep in mind that all of this happened before the Kindle hit the market, which means I've watched the process repeated in the self-publishing field as well. First the Kindle opened up new tactics and ebooks boomed, then tools like KDP select arrived and shifted their playing field and offer new tactics.

People set up their business to take advantage of those tactics, then found themselves losing ground when Amazon changed the fee structures, moving away from books borrowed (which favoured shorter works) to pages read in order to determine pay-outs. Folks who had built their business around the former structure had to pivot and change their tactics, and some couldn't do it fast enough to stay in the game.

Heck, I've watched this happen in publishing generally as well. The venerable tools for getting a book out there and connecting with readers are muddied by the arrival of social media and blogging, which changed dynamics and started a wave of "you must blog/tweet/Facebook" conversations with editors and agents.

New technological tools disrupt the industry, opening up new tactics for achieving your goals as a writer. The problems come when people confuse those tools and tactics for a long-term, unchanging strategy.

ON TOOLS, TACTICS, STRATEGY, & DISRUPTIVE TECHNOLOGY

In really simple terms, strategy is the overall vision of what you're trying to do. Tactics are the short-term plans you use to get there.

In 2009's *BookLife*, Jeff VanderMeer's outstanding book on the strategies and survival tips for the writing life, he breaks down the basic problem between tactical and strategic thinking: writers work organically, which means they shy away from lists and goals. This leaves them thinking tactically, on a project-to-project horizon, instead of having a long term strategy about where they want to go.

Or, to put it another way, most writers can happily tell you what they're working on *now*. Some can give you an idea of what they'll do with it once the project is done. Very few can tell you how today's project builds towards a long-term goal, five years down the line.

In short, writers suck at strategy, and this is a problem in a world where the tools and tactics keep changing.

It's an even bigger problem in a world where the tools you're using for some tactical approaches are owned by someone else, and are vulnerable to sudden changes based upon their strategies rather than yours.

Tactics are implemented in the service of long-term strategy, but you've got to have a high-level view or you're doing things for the sake of doing things. A general doesn't deploy their forces to take a beach because they want the beach particularly, but because it's the best possible staging ground for the next phase of their plan and part of a long-term strategy for winning the damn war.

TACTICS AND DIGITAL DISRUPTION

What's interesting about living in the age of digital disruption is the tendency for people to produce tools that make new tactics viable.

There is nothing particularly new about Patreon's core approach. Artist have always had the option of going to their fans directly in order to monetise their art. Wealthy patrons supported great artists when it was seen as a sign of status, and professional street performers rely on the same engagement with passers-by to earn an income.

What limited that idea, in terms of many artists making a viable amount of money, was access to enough fans with sufficient wealth and desire to support your work. If you weren't doing something a wealthy patron liked, or your art wasn't flashy enough to capture the attention of commuters as they crossed your patch, the option was closed to you.

Patreon took the same theory as busking on a busy street corner, except the internet allowed you to access fans around the globe and you could set up a recurring charge on their credit card instead of asking for a little change.

Suddenly a tactic most artists had disregarded was viable in a big way, simply because a digital tool existed to make it easy and viable. This same thing is true of the ebook boom, which conquered the distribution problem that made self-publishing a substandard option for most writers.

NEW TACTICS AREN'T NEW STRATEGIES

The problem with the emergence of a new tool, which opens up a previously unviable tactic, is the ease with which it becomes assumed that it's an unchanging, long-term strategy. Our approach to making an income becomes tailored to the toolkit we're working with, and it feels like the rug is pulled out from underneath you the moment the tool changes.

I'm yet to come across a tool aimed at creators that hasn't changed and evolved as it matured. They're all owned by companies pursuing their own long-term strategies and applying different tactics in order to achieve those goals. Patron was four years old when they proposed changes to their fee structure, which is roughly about the point that change starts to hit.

Thing is, good tools are seductive because the tactics they open up are working so well. The good tools built by people looking to monetise creative work will always present themselves like long-term strategies because, as VanderMeer notes, they're working with creative-types who don't excel at strategic thinking and just want to get through the next ten minutes instead of the next ten years.

Moreover, the people building the tools are very good at encouraging this kind of thinking because that's part of their strategy. When you're making a tool, it's only valuable if you have people using it and encouraging others to lease those tools in order to replicate previous success.

All tools evolve once you've proven the concept. Once upon a time we hammered shit in with rocks, then someone invented the hammer and we build different kinds of buildings because the tools improved. Then someone invented the nail gun.

The problem, in the online space, is that selling the tool directly is frequently a substandard option. Tools from Patreon to Adobe Photoshop are more interested in renting the tools out for a monthly fee or a percentage of each transaction. This requires long-term buy in, and it pays to make it harder to embrace other tools or tactics.

This is frequently subtle. Having delved on the indie side of things for the first time in a while, I'm consistently impressed by Amazon's ability to make it look like the upload process isn't really finished until I've broken down and put my books in their subscription program, forcing me to accept restrictions on how and where my books can be sold.

Similarly, while I ultimately decided against a Patreon, I'm consistently impressed by the way they sell their services to those who have expressed an interest. Their communications team does a great job of making it sound like the best possible option for diversifying your income as a creative.

It's hard not to get suckered in, particularly when there are early adopters who are doing great and the approach feel revolutionary. I'm pretty sure every creative has one experience with it – I learned it the hard-way in my RPG ebook publishing days, when the consequences of building my tactics around the habits of just one sales site bit me in the ass just as I got my press established — but the response when you realise things has changed is the important part.

Railing at the folks who changed the tool feels great in the short-term, and may even have results and get things reversed for a time, but even if that happens it's never quite the same. First, you've just seen the shift in their thinking, and reversing the decision doesn't change the problem they're trying to solve. Second, the customers who are engaging with you using the tool are similarly aware that it's not the same anymore, especially when they feel like they've been burned.

This means you no longer get to make tactical decisions on autopilot. Folks are left with three options: learn to think strategically and adapt their tactics as required; accept that they'll do what they've always done and there will probably be less income; or give up because it's just too hard to keep going with diminishing returns.

Only one of those is a truly sustainable option, but it's also the hardest of them if you're not used to thinking in those terms.

2018 COMMENTARY

I shied away from including 2017 posts in this collection, but a handful of my regular readers specifically requested its inclusion. In many ways, this is the culmination of several things I'd been considering since I started really focusing on writing strategies and tactics in my essay, *You Don't Want To Be Published*, several years earlier.

While Patreon backed away from their proposed changes pretty quickly, the damage was largely done. One of the key tricks with getting people to mistakenly thinking of digital tools as a core strategy is keep them thinking you're on their side.

Links

This list contains the web adresses for the original posts and any major references contained within. All these links are current at time of printing.

The Nine Business Mantras of the Cranky Writer

- Original Post:
  http://www.petermball.com/the-nine-business-mantras-of-a-cranky-writer/

You Don't Want To Be Published

- Original Post:
  http://www.petermball.com/you-dont-want-to-be-published/

Focus On the Mountain, Not the Map

- Original Post: http://www.petermball.com/focus-on-the-mountain-not-the-map/

Writing, Budgeting, and Shame

- Original Post: http://www.petermball.com/writing-budgeting-and-shame/

Let's Be Clear: I Know Fuck-All About Writing and Publishing

- Original Post: http://www.petermball.com/lets-be-clear-i-know-fuck-all-about-writing-and-publishing/
- Writer Beware: https://www.sfwa.org/other-resources/for-authors/writer-beware/

How To Process Publishing Advice, Part One: Use What Works

- Original Post: http://www.petermball.com/how-i-process-writing-advice/

How To Process Writing Advice, Part Two: Diversity Your Sources

- Original Post: http://www.petermball.com/how-to-process-writing-advice-redux-diversify-your-sources/

There Is Nothing Surprising About A Writer Getting Rejected (Even J.K. Rowling)

- Original Post: http://www.petermball.com/there-is-nothing-surprising-about-a-writer-getting-rejected-even-jk-rowling/

5 Reasons Rejection Letters Are Actually Awesome

- Original Post: http://www.petermball.com/5-reasons-rejection-letters-are-actually-awesome/

Yes, You Are Wasting Your Time As a Writer

- Original Post: http://www.petermball.com/yes-you-are-wasting-your-time-as-a-writer/

The First Rule of Write Club

- Original Post:

http://www.petermball.com/the-first-rule-of-write-club-is-talk-about-write-club/

The Incredible Sucker-Punch of Success

- Original Post: http://www.petermball.com/the-incredible-sucker-punch-of-success/

Networking Tips for Reclusive, Introverted Writer-Types

- Original Post: http://www.petermball.com/networking-tips-for-reclusive-introverted-writer-types/
- Kim Weisel's Advice on Working the Room on Ink.Inc: https://www.inc.com/kimberly-weisul/how-to-work-a-room-the-only-strategy-you-need.html

How to get the Most out of an SF Con as an (Introverted) Emerging Writer

- Original Post: http://www.petermball.com/how-to-get-the-most-out-of-a-sf-con-as-an-introverted-emerging-writer/

Al Snow's Advice for SF Writers

- Original Essay: https://www.apex-magazine.com/al-snows-advice-for-sf-writers/

Patreon, Tools, Tactics, and Strategy

- Original Post: http://www.petermball.com/patreon-tools-tactics-and-strategy/

About the Author

Peter M Ball has been teaching students about writing and publishing for 20 years. He's published more than fifty short stories and six novellas, along with essays, RPG material, articles, and poetry.

He's previously taught creative writing at Griffith University and the Queensland Writers Centre, spent five years as the manager of the Australian Writers Marketplace, and convened four GenreCon writing conferences. He's currently working on a PhD about the poetics of series fiction.

When not teaching, studying, and writing stories, he runs Brain Jar Press and geeks out about comic books, B-movies, roleplaying games, and superhero cartoons.

Peter can be found online at:
www.petermball.com

- facebook.com/PeterMBallAuthor
- twitter.com/petermball
- instagram.com/petermball

www.ingramcontent.com/pod-product-compliance
Lightning Source LLC
Chambersburg PA
CBHW020324010526
44107CB00054B/1972